D0230019

IN WAR HEROES WAKE

Written by

Roger and Sandra Downton

Traveller's Joy Publishing

Published by Traveller's Joy Publishing

www.cockleshellheroes.co.uk

ISBN 0-9550166-0-6
Printed by Xpress Printing, Poole, BH12 3LL.
Tel: 01202 717322

SYNOPSIS

In December 1942, twelve men set out to execute a daring and imaginative attack on enemy shipping lying in the docks of Bordeaux. There unfolded a war story of great human sacrifice, courage, danger, tenacity and achievement. The mission was called Operation Frankton, and the men involved became known as the legendary Cockleshell Heroes. At the outset of the Operation, a succession of disasters left only four men to continue with the mission. Eventually, after a gruelling, covert canoe journey at night in the depths of winter, they successfully planted their specially designed magnetic 'limpet' mines on the enemy ships moored in the harbour of Bordeaux. Just two men – Major Hasler and Marine Bill Sparks - came back alive.

This is not only the story of the Cockleshell Heroes and their famous Second World War raid, but the tale of two ordinary civilians, Roger and Sandra Downton from Poole in Dorset who, inspired by the heroism and daring exploits of the Cockleshell Heroes, retraced, with very little knowledge or experience of canoeing, the course of the daring mission. This absorbing account of Roger and Sandra's research, oddball training programme, adaptation of more 'economic equipment' and clothing, and their quest to raise sponsorship are all light-heartedly explained and delicately interwoven together with the gripping story of the original men of Operation Frankton. Paddling in the wake of those commandos, our intrepid married couple set off up the perilous River Gironde. In a canoe, lovingly called 'Sardine', follow their frightening struggle with the ferocious currents, the uncertainty of where they would stop overnight, and the peregrination that took them past the famous picturesque wine regions of France, eventually culminating in their triumphant arrival at the scene of the attack in the splendid harbour of Bordeaux. Their challenging and enlightening experiences make interesting and exciting reading.

Other work by the same author

PART ONE ORDERS

Set in 1969 Northern Ireland at the beginning of the troubles and
through internment in 1971.
A gritty and powerful story portrayed from the foot soldiers
perspective and their interaction with the ordinary people who
were thrown into a maelstrom of violence and hatred.
Action, danger, romance, humour.

If you were there, or ever wondered what it was like, this is the
definitive account.

FOREWORD

by

General Sir Robert Pascoe, KCB, MBE,
late of the Royal Green Jackets

Everyone of a certain age must have heard something about the Cockleshell Heroes of World War II, even if only as a result of seeing the film of that name. A dozen brave and determined men paddled flimsy canoes into enemy occupied France to carry out a costly but successful raid against German shipping and registered a British success at a time when there was not much to raise our morale.

There are not many people today however who would think of following in the wake of those men and even fewer people would prove able to carry such an enterprise through to a successful conclusion.

Roger and Sandra Downton did just that and this book is a readable account of the planning and execution of their expedition while, at the same time, refreshing our memories about the wartime operation.

Roger served in the 1st Battalion of The Royal Green Jackets when I was its Commanding Officer in the early 1970's and he and Sandra are active in various of our Regimental reunions.

I enjoyed reading their no frills narrative which carries the reader along at a good pace and creates the desire to find out what happened next. They have set down an interesting record of their enterprising, testing and rewarding journey following the paddle strokes of those real Cockleshell Heroes.

CONTENTS

BACKGROUND

INTRODUCTION

PLANNING AND PREPARATION

THE JOURNEY

SUMMING UP

DEDICATION

To Bill Sparks and his comrades from Operation Frankton
who guided us safely to our destination.

THE REASON FOR OPERATION FRANKTON

Nineteen forty two was becoming a shaky time for the allies, Singapore had fallen, the Japanese were knocking on the gates of India, Rommel had given the Desert Rats a pasting in Egypt and taken Tobruk, many casualties had been sustained in Malaya, the Russians were getting a hammering, and the Americans had been attacked in the Pacific. Enemy ships were operating almost unchallenged from the Far East to German occupied European ports, in particular Bordeaux. Items such as rubber, tin, tungsten, and animal and vegetable oil were moving from Japan, through Bordeaux to Germany and Italy, and were obviously vital commodities for the enemy's war machine. Manufacturing materials and weapons were also moving virtually unopposed in the opposite direction. In the Atlantic, allied merchant shipping was suffering big losses as a result of a purge by German U boats. A solution was necessary, but not easy to find ….. committing the overstretched British Navy and submarines to attack the cargo ships in the Bay of Biscay was out of the question. Air strikes, although within range, had been ruled out because RAF deployment was already to its limit, plus the fact that at the time, targeting equipment and skills were still primitive and inaccurate. In order for enemy ships to be destroyed in Bordeaux, and to end German complacency, it would mean bombing the whole harbour, causing a great loss of French lives. Such action would have an adverse influence on public opinion in France and the free French abroad. Combined land, sea and air attacks requiring thousands of troops and support units, again with the possibility of sustaining many allied military and civilian casualties, were also a no, no.* With all these gloomy facts in mind, the Combined Operations Examination Committee put their thinking caps on, their egg heads together, and began to study the possibilities of an alternative means of attack. As luck would have it, a brilliant idea to attack the enemy ships using a small flotilla of specialist men and canoes was conceived and proposed by a certain creative boating and canoeing enthusiast, Major 'Blondie' Hasler. Details of his ingenious idea were presented in a letter, signed by its most fervent supporter, Louis Mountbatten, and fell on the desks of the influential.

Comparing this predicament to present times, nothing much seems to have changed on the front line of battle, wherever it may be. Ironically, even with all the modern technology that has produced sophisticated weapons, electronic wizardry and pinpoint accuracy, the world's leading armies still become bogged down and embroiled in bloody, endless wars that are massively expensive, not only in financial cost but also in valuable resources, property and innumerable lives.

A BIT ABOUT US

I am Roger Downton and I live with my wife Sandra in the seaside town of Poole in Dorset. We both work in the music and entertainment industry. We love adventure and outdoor activities such as walking and cycling, both of which have taken us over some breathtaking, beautiful expanses of the planet. In order to gain access to some of these wondrous sights, we have endured excruciatingly wet, dry, cold, searingly hot, humid, windy, mind and body numbing, rugged, tough and taxing terrain. We've dragged our mountain bikes over miles of volcanic lava strewn mountain ranges to watch magnificent eagles soar, and hauled our backpacks, soaking wet, along thundery cliff tops to be rewarded by dynamic crashing seas and steep, heart stopping rugged coastlines. Together, for five months, Sandra and I roughed it in the blazing hot, deadly animal and insect infested outback and rain forests of Australia. Transport and living accommodation during our exploration of that rugged, dry, dusty continent was a small, charming old banger of a camper van that occasionally subjected us to some potentially life threatening mechanical malfunctions. We hoped, perhaps naively, that our numerous experiences would have qualified and toughened us for the Cockleshell adventure. However, we discovered that it required different disciplines and stamina. Sandra is an avid swimmer, and in pursuit of this passion, will plunge into water that stops me, due to the low temperature, at ankle depth. I, on the other hand, can plod along for quite some time in friendly water conditions, practising my one and only means of propulsion, the breast stroke. This, I alternate with floating on my back, how I imagine I would end up in an emergency situation, floundering around till help arrived, or I drifted with the current to a friendly shore. From an early age, Sandra had always enjoyed 'messing about in boats'. Her ambition as a teenager was to sail round the world, until one day she ventured out of Poole Harbour in a friend's yacht and was promptly sick! In complete contrast, my grounding for our expedition, was six years working as a speciality cabaret artiste on board many luxury cruise liners. Therefore, the slight transition from palatial cruise ship to simple canoe was hardly noticeable!

COMPARED TO US

Many of the men who volunteered, and eventually took part in Operation Frankton, could not swim, and in fact never learned. Paradoxically, some of the men who could not swim on the surface became very competent underwater 'frogmen'. Marine Eric Fisher, who could just about float on the surface, became really efficient underwater. Conversely, tough, husky Ellery, a fine surface swimmer, hated even the thought of being submerged. With that detail in mind, my lack of ability in the swimming department was never considered a problem on our adventure.

Our Spartan traits led us to buy a canoe, but although we like to take the tougher, challenging route in most pursuits, we are by no means masochistically inclined, or prone to indulging in any unnecessarily dangerous, extreme, or punishingly painful things. That includes volunteering for missions behind enemy lines.

An objective is very important to us. Rambling, cycling, or canoeing around in circles for no reason is simply just plain boring, therefore it is worth struggling a rough course, however small, to reach a destination that promises the reward of something interesting.

AN INTERESTING LINK

An interesting discovery for me was that the first person to explore the military possibilities of the two-man canoe was Lieutenant Roger Courtney of the Kings Royal Rifle Corps, the second battalion of the Green Jackets. This is significant because I served with the 43rd & 52nd Ox and Bucks Light Infantry, the first battalion of the Green Jackets ..... a spiritual, if tenuous, link.

MAJOR 'BLONDIE' HASLER - BACKGROUND AND TRAINING

In 1942, Major Hasler was twenty eight years old, six feet tall, athletically built and with very thin, pale, red-gold hair and a matching moustache. These attributes had earned him the name 'Blondie'. Since a young boy, he had been passionate about boats. With a friend, at the age of twelve, he built his first canvas covered two-seater canoe in which he learned the basics of navigation, and at fourteen, he designed and built a sailing boat on his own. He made many single-handed trips around Southsea, Hayling Island, Chichester and the marshy backwaters of Portsmouth. He was able to look after himself and would often be away from home for days, spending his nights alone on the bleak mudflats. His mother 'knew he would always turn up', as she said, when he disappeared on Operation Frankton. As an ambitious seaman, he was a tenacious individualist and in 1941 he wrote a paper on attacking ships by canoe. So it was without any surprise that when Mountbatten gave permission and approval for Hasler's application to form his own special canoe unit, he set out on a strict self training course. Night after night Hasler went out alone in his canoe practising 'stealth' to be able to get to a target undetected. He went on long walks, swam every day and took revolver and other forms of weapon training. He designed a cradle device for lowering the canoes from the deck of the submarine and down into the water. All this knowledge was passed on to his men who went through rigorous physical and tactical training. The crews were sent out alone in the Solent at night to hone in their navigational techniques, and spent many hours on movement with stealth, map reading, camouflage and concealment, dealing with a capsized canoe, repairing a damaged canoe, and basically all the techniques that would be required to succeed.

Major 'Blondie' Hasler, the creator and leader of Operation Frankton, personally hand-picked the twelve men that he used on the mission, but it's interesting to note that none of them had any previous knowledge or understanding of boating whatsoever, including the officers and N.C.O's, and therefore it was down to Major Hasler to teach them all the rudiments. His intuition and natural instincts were his main selection tools. The criteria he set out in his appeal was for 'volunteers for hazardous service', 'men eager to engage the enemy', 'indifferent to personal safety', 'free of strong family ties'.

EMPATHY

Major Hasler's childhood is something that I can relate to because, from the age of twelve, I spent many days and nights, in all kinds of weather, hiking over the bleak tracks of Dartmoor and Exmoor. Compared to today, I had very little in the way of survival equipment or clothes simply because, in those days, it just wasn't available, and it really didn't occur to me that it was necessary. I would sleep rough, with no tent or sleeping bag, finding shelter beside the large, plentiful boulders on the hills, or behind a dry stone wall. I had a small, ex-Army shoulder bag in which I had my food supply ..... a box of Kellogg's Cornflakes. This I would mix with water from a stream. As far as clothing was concerned, I wore a vest, pants, shirt, knitted cardigan, tweed jacket, knee length wool socks, leather shoes, and short flannel trousers. I also wore a snake buckled school belt, with a small leather pouch attached, and this contained a small compass, homemade map, clasp knife, police whistle, and some string. When I'd had enough, I would find a red 'phone box (I spent the night in one once) and make a reverse charge call to my doting parents, give them my location, and they would happily set out from Bournemouth to collect me.

BILL SPARKS

Bill Sparks was born in the East End of London in 1922, and joined the Marines at the beginning of the Second World War, aged seventeen. He was a tall, lanky, curly haired jolly cockney of twenty when he became a Cockleshell Hero, sharing the same canoe as Major Hasler. Before the formation of the Cockleshell Heroes, he served for two years in HMS Renown, and whilst stationed in Iceland, he fell into the freezing sea, caught bronchial pneumonia, and as a direct result, was dogged with chest problems in later life.

MAJOR HASLER'S LEADERSHIP QUALITIES

Major Hasler was a natural leader, attributed with the necessary vital qualities for his role. He was conscientious, tough, single-minded and ruthless, but was careful to exercise the correct proportion of fairness. He also had the 'courage of his convictions' which gave his men complete faith and commitment. His relationship with them was kept at a respectful distance. He had nothing in common socially or intellectually with any of them. The old adage, 'familiarity breeds contempt', played an important role in Hasler's leadership strategy. He was superior to them, he knew it, they understood it, and that fact bolstered them with confidence. All his men, without exception, respected him for those qualities; it made them feel secure, they trusted his judgement, and therefore would follow him with total, unfaltering dedication.

BILL'S POINT OF VIEW

Bill Sparks told me that he was fortunate to be in the same canoe as Major Hasler, and that his commander had no misgivings or doubts whatsoever with regard to his plan. Bill knew that Hasler, in keeping with his nature, had complete faith in the integrity of his creation, Operation Frankton, and in his dogged determination and ability to carry it off. Sparks said that having a commander with that amount of blind confidence gave him an almost certain chance of returning in tact.

THOSE WHO PASSED MUSTER

The men who were chosen to take part in Operation Frankton were a true cross section of bold, fearless British stock, and typical of that era. They possessed a burning sense of duty, discipline, respect, courtesy, and were willing to fight tyranny, and if necessary, suffer and pay the ultimate sacrifice for the freedom of their country, fellow men, women and children.

Major H.G. 'Blondie' Hasler
The epitome of a dedicated Operation Commander from Hampshire.

Marine W.E. Sparks (Ned to his mates)
The wiry, tough, chirpy cockney.

Sergeant Samuel Wallace
An engaging, cheerful, professional soldier from Dublin.

Marine Robert Ewart
From simple farm stock, a keen, courageous Glaswegian.

Corporal A.F. Laver
A quiet, most dependable man, a fighter with initiative from Barnet.

Marine W.H. Mills
A spirited, altruistic, and likable chap from Kettering.

Corporal G.J. Sheard
A witty, tenacious fellow who hailed from Devonshire.

Marine D. Moffat
A lively, enthusiastic character from Halifax, Yorkshire, but born in Belfast.

Lieutenant J.W. Mackinnon
A gallant, first-class, rough-and-ready officer from Glasgow.

Marine J. Conway
A strong, quiet young man, quick witted, loved horses, from Stockport, Cheshire.

Marine W.A. Ellery
A fine swimmer and reliable comrade from London.

Marine E. Fisher
A fine young man, non-swimmer but with plenty of guts from West Bromwich.

THE BIRTH OF THE 'SARDINE'

We thought that buying a canoe would be a straightforward task, but how wrong we were. Arriving pea green and soaking wet behind the ears at the canoe warehouse, we encountered the gushing, formulated, jargonistic canoe speak of the sales chappie. He was quite charming, helpful, and certainly knew his onions. This was definitely an esoteric situation, and thinking on our feet, we told him what we had in mind and what we were about to attempt, and decided to trust his obvious knowledgeable guidance and judgement to steer us to the correct and most suitable craft for our specialist requirements. Our fundamental request was that we wanted a canoe for one person in the front and one in the back with some kind of waterproof cover ….. like the Cockleshell Heroes. With a wry smile and knowing look, he took us into the huge store room. There were racks and racks of canoes and kayaks of all different shapes, sizes and colours ….. little stubby jobs for storming down white water rivers, and narrow pencil thin types with agonising looking seats the shape of those terribly sharp, bottom impaling racing bike saddles. Wanting to appear confident, we approached a fine looking bottle green craft, the type I remember seeing in cowboy films as a boy, being used by the Red Indians. "Wow, I like this one," said Sandra enthusiastically. "I can picture us paddling along in this." The salesman politely explained, "This is a canoe in which one adopts a semi-kneeling position using a single paddle. It's very heavy and you need to have a certain amount of experience, strength and handling skills." We could see him discretely assessing our age, fitness and sizes, whereupon he delicately moved us from the kayak to something more suitable. Following him through the aisles of tall steel racks that house the various craft, we arrived at a section of vertically stacked, vacuum packed in what appeared to be giant condoms, tastefully coloured canoes. All agreed on the turquoise one; he adeptly removed it from the rack and laid it before us. Like two expectant parents, we stood by as he removed the womb-like protective sheath, whilst we witnessed the birth and first sight of the 'Sardine'.

Then it was accessories time ….. which of the plethora of paddles in all weights, sizes and designs did we want, which life-jacket, and which spray deck? Once again, we followed his judgement which inevitably proved to be correct. By tilting the front passenger's seat as far forward as it would go, we managed to slide eighty per cent of the canoe inside our estate car. The rest protruded from the back, so I strapped the tail gate down on to the canoe deck with rope which I then secured to the towing hitch. It was obvious at this early stage that we would need to purchase a roof rack.

Home we sped with our new acquisition. We were now the proud owners of a canoe.

NAMING THE OPERATION FRANKTON CANOES

At first the canoes were called 'Cockles'. After a while, and as experimentation influenced design progress, they became historically known as 'Cockleshells'. For easy reference, Major Hasler gave all six of them names: Catfish, Crayfish, Conger, Cuttlefish, Coalfish and Cachalot. We affectionately christened ours, Sardine.

COCKLESHELL CANOE CONSTRUCTION

The type of canoe used on the Operation had a ply board bottom with wooden runners enabling it to be dragged over sandy mud or shingle. The sides were made of canvas and the top deck was again ply board. They were sixteen feet long, twenty eight inches wide, and eleven inches high. The foredeck was fitted with a collapsible breakwater to assist deflection of water in rough conditions and when pitching into waves. The cockpit area where they sat (on torturous wooden seats with no sympathetic shaping for the human frame) was covered by a waterproof canvas cover. This was held together along the centre with spring clips that would sympathetically release if they were to capsize. When the Cockleshells were erected, they would just fit through the torpedo hatch of a submarine. They weighed roughly ninety pounds and could take two men with one hundred and fifty pounds of equipment.

A pleasing synchronicity for us to discover during our research was that the actual canoes used for the Operation were made in our home town of Poole, at Parkstone Joinery.

THE FAITHFUL 'SARDINE' SPECIFICATIONS

The 'Sardine' is a two-man, rigid, moulded plastic canoe. The open cockpit area has two comfortable moulded seats and is covered by two waterproof canvas spray decks. Two strips of Velcro join the front canoeist's canvas spray deck apron to the one at the rear. This makes an almost watertight seal when pulled over the cockpit rim and tightened with an elastic toggle. In exceptionally rough conditions, or when water was continually washing over the deck, I found that it began to seep its way through the Velcro join and irritatingly drip on to my legs. Three feet shorter than the original Cockleshells, the Sardine is thirteen feet long, but is wider by five inches making it a stable thirty three inches. Empty, she weighs in at sixty three pounds, twenty seven less than the Cockleshells. We did start weighing all our kit out on the patio using the bathroom scales but gave that up because it became clear that whatever we took was ultimately determined by the available space ….. so we just thought light, minimal, and kept to the bare essentials. In fact we had roughly 100 pounds of kit on board.

INTRODUCTION

Why did we decide to attempt the trip? It would seem that a series of fateful events led us up to it. As a boy, I had been fascinated by the film 'The Cockleshell Heroes', subsequently read the book, and then many years later, had the privilege to meet Bill Sparks, the last living survivor of Operation Frankton, at his home in Alfriston. These events were to have a lasting and profound effect. After another lapse of years, Sandra, my lovely wife, and I were in Gosport when we noticed a newspaper bill board declaring that poor old Bill Sparks had died. On the way home, we saw a second-hand canoe for sale. That prompted us to research the canoe market and ultimately buy a two-man canoe ….. 'The Sardine'. Prompted by watching a 60th anniversary documentary about the mission, from my comfortable armchair, downing a few glasses of red, I said to Sandra, "Shall we retrace the steps of the Cockleshell Heroes in our own canoe?" Romanticising the dangerous deed, her rationality also clouded by the same red wine, she agreed, and that was it, we were unstoppable. To give the project more substance, or kudos, and because we thought it would be of public interest, we contacted the BBC regional TV and the local Daily Echo which both offered to do a feature. A date was booked for a photo shoot in Poole Harbour and so we were committed, there was no going back. Once people, in particular our friends, had read or viewed what we were going to do, we couldn't chicken out. We felt no fear of what we were about to attempt, even 'though many of our friends expressed their concern that we had very little experience and that we had been given no formal training. Everyone seemed to be preoccupied with the fact that we hadn't been doing 'Eskimo rolls', apparently in order to prepare us for what everyone seemed to believe was the inevitable ….. our capsize. What they didn't understand was, that with the amount of gear we had stuffed into our canoe, and the breadth of its beam, there was absolutely no chance of us getting it back upright, as some of the original commandos had found to their tragic cost. However, whenever we were out paddling in Poole Harbour, we would verbally go over and over our capsize escape routine. This was usually prompted by the wash of a passing ferry or other speeding craft which brought home to us our smallness and vulnerability to even the slightest of waves. We had decided, as safety announcements predictably and prosaically quote, 'in the unlikely event', that once completely upside-down and submerged, having gulped in as much air as possible on our way over, our immediate action would be to release the canvas decking from the canoe, and with it still attached to our waists like skirts, we would then calmly and without panic - in theory – slide ourselves out and make for the surface. Naively, my main concern was the loss of any, or all, of our belongings and equipment. Indeed, during my years working aboard cruise ships, one of the staff's preoccupations and verbal games during boring times (when the passengers, thankfully, were confined to their cabins with seasickness) was trying to decide, if the ship began to sink, which item any of us valued enough to risk rushing down to our cabin, defying a watery death, to retrieve, before making for the lifeboat. My most precious possession was my guitar. At least I could play it in the lifeboat and take our minds off starvation, eating each other, sharks eating us, dehydration and impending delirium as we drifted aimlessly in the ocean awaiting rescue.

Our only canoe experience had been a few tranquil sunny days paddling around Poole Harbour in Dorset, dragging it ashore on one of the island's sandy beaches to enjoy a relaxing picnic. However, Sandra and I had bigger ambitions with this primitive form of transport. Armed with little experience and a wholly inadequate knowledge of boating - and a waterproof navigation chart – we crossed the English Channel and drove 350 miles to Pointe de Grave in western France where we slid our heavily laden two-man canoe into the murky brown Gironde River estuary, and set off towards the city of Bordeaux, situated almost a hundred miles ahead. Our intention was to pay tribute to the legendary W.W.11 Cockleshell Heroes of Operation Frankton by retracing their course. Their orders were to destroy enemy shipping lying in Bordeaux Harbour. Only two men of the original ten survived to tell the tale. Two drowned in the ferocious tidal races, and six were caught and mercilessly tortured before being shot. With the story of their daring and arduous exploits from the book and the film fresh in our minds, we innocently paddled in their wake, visiting all the spots on the river bank where they hid and camouflaged themselves amongst the reeds during the daylight hours under the noses of the swarming murderous Nazis. Our naivety turned out to be our greatest survival kit, for if, beforehand, we had been totally aware of the latent dangers lurking in La Gironde, we most probably would not have entertained the trip. It feels rewarding to have succeeded in our task, and we congratulate ourselves for completing the challenge, and it is especially all the more significant for us being in our late middle-aged period of life. We had hoped for a good tidal current to help us in our endeavour, but hadn't anticipated such a strong, churning and temperamental one. In a capsize situation, we would have been swiftly swept along by the current with very little hope of swimming to the safety of the shore. To compound it, when we saw the many old rotten pointed wooden posts, sharp rusty wire, logs and other obstacles revealed at low tide, it became blatantly obvious that there was a strong possibility that if we had found ourselves in the water, we would surely have become snagged by our legs, clothing or any submerged portion of our bodies, held fast, and dragged under by the fierce current. Any thought of grabbing hold of the slippery smooth under body of the canoe in such conditions was completely out of the question.

THE SPIRITS OF OPERATION FRANKTON

The idea of a middle-aged married couple retracing a hazardous and dangerous wartime operation wasn't a spur of the moment decision or overnight plan. As mentioned, it had been smouldering latently and subconsciously for many, many years, and was finally ignited by a combination of events. Our motivation was not to set ourselves a mindless challenge, but to go on a pilgrimage and to pay homage to the gallant men of Operation Frankton. Above all, we truly believe that the spirits of the protagonists in Operation Frankton played a large part in our exciting endeavour. The presence of those who had died during, or since taking part in the Operation were like an aura around us and our canoe. We seemed at times to be insulated from reality, travelling within a gossamer thin bubble, bouncing us away from any potential danger. To some, an ancient archaeological site will produce an unexplained energy or power, and to us, the area and places connected to the Cockleshell Heroes have the same mysterious atmosphere.

OUR RESEARCH

Most of our research was from written or video documentation, but one other source was prompted by an advert on the internet, asking for participants to join in a 'Cockleshell Heroes' guided walk in Portsmouth, Hampshire. The organisation offered to take us to all the actual sites where the men of Operation Frankton had undergone their training. On the day of the walk, accompanied by drizzling rain, and suitably dressed in our waterproof jackets and leggings, we arrived at the entrance to Southsea Pier. We were surprised but encouraged to see that around twenty other people had turned up despite the dire weather conditions, looking enthusiastic and eager to take part. Whilst waiting for the guide to arrive, we casually acquainted ourselves with some of the other members of the party. It transpired that apart from us and a couple of other Cockleshell enthusiasts, the rest of the people were regular organised theme ramblers who had visited and walked many different historic sites throughout the country. Our guide was a charming elderly lady, well-spoken, direct, tough and definitely of the old school brigade. It was refreshing to discover in her dialogue that she had no time for fatuous political correctness. She possessed an obvious passion for the subject and the men involved. She spoke of them with an endearing familiarity, as though they were her own 'boys'. It came to light that she was retiring after many, many years of walking and talking the Cockleshell route and that we were to be her last group. We all paid her the three pounds a head and she set off at a good pace, like a mother hen with us all flocking behind. During our comfortable but damp ramble within the close proximity of the Southsea promenade, she would occasionally halt us at the various relevant places and narrate in detail when, where, why, and to whom something had taken place. Unfortunately her voice was rather weak, worn out by the years of trying to project above the wind, sea, and traffic noise. It proved difficult at times to hear every word she was saying, causing some on the periphery of the group to become irritable and call for her to speak up. Their whinging made it worse because we missed even more information under the noise of their complaints. Clutched tightly under her arm was a large, blue, hardback office file containing all her facts and information associated with Operation Frankton. There were maps of the attack marked with felt-tip, and faded newspaper cuttings with black and white pictures depicting the two surviving servicemen regaled with their medals alongside various fawning dignitaries. She led us on to Canoe Lake, located just two hundred yards opposite Southsea Pier, which still serves that purpose. She fascinated us with the fact that during the beginning of the war, the Germans dropped a bomb right in the centre of it, thus increasing its depth. Ironically, she continued, "They couldn't have done a better job because it transformed it into an ideal location for the men of Operation Frankton to practice their various techniques, such as placing their limpet mines underwater." Another interesting detail that we learned from her was that Major Hasler was a strict disciplinarian and task master, and that he regularly made his men run barefoot along the pebble strewn shoreline. Apparently, this was to harden their feet and toughen their endurance. She seemed to wallow in any agonising, gory, suffering details, and always qualified it with, "These weren't the mamby pamby youth of today, they were tough, fighting men who were prepared to give the ultimate sacrifice for their country." From the pejorative murmuring amongst the group, vociferously expressing their negative opinions of today's youth, it was obvious that the majority agreed with her.

MORE ENLIGHTENMENT

We moved on through the drizzling rain and wind to the relative sanctuary of the Rose Garden. The party approached the garden entrance, consisting of two tall brick gate posts on which hung heavy black wrought iron gates. Before passing through the gate, our guide drew our attention to a metal plaque on one of the gate posts with an engraved commemorative inscription to the memory of those who had died on the mission. The beautifully manicured garden had an air of tranquillity, and was surrounded on all sides by a fifteen foot high rustic red brick wall. We shuffled reverently, speaking in hushed tones, around the half an acre or so of garden where the men lived during their training, or rather camped out in very Spartan conditions. As their mission was top secret, they were most furtive, didn't light fires in the garden, and were extra careful not to be noticed. Rather contradicting the need for secrecy, she went on to tell us that Hasler had created a fast marching pace specifically for his men. They were often seen marching swiftly along the sea front, and their style soon acquired a nickname from the locals, 'The Southsea Stroll'. Their rapid marching pace was of particular interest to me, having been a soldier in the Green Jackets Light Infantry and very much used to a fast marching pace. Our last stop, the Royal Marines Museum, was rather disappointing. "All the details of Operation Frankton have been locked away in the volts!" was the curt reply to our obvious question, after which the attendant went back to his important mobile telephone conversation. This reminded us of the fact that there is a memorial to the Cockleshell Heroes and Operation Frankton at the Marine Barracks in Hamworthy, Poole, but as it is contained within the camp, we have so far been unable to gain access.

REFLECTION

Everyone thanked the guide for such an absorbing and informative tour, wished her good luck in her well-earned retirement, and went their separate ways. Sandra and I decided to return on our own to the Rose Garden, sit on one of the benches, and absorb the serene atmosphere. We imagined, as best we could, what it must have been like for the men ..... their emotions during their preparation, excitement, nervous anticipation of not knowing what lay before them, wanting to just get on with it. The tougher the training, the closer the bonding of their little group would have been. Sandra, knowing that I'd served in the Infantry as a Rifleman and had experienced combat alongside fellow comrades, asked my opinion with regard to the training and lead up to the Operation. I imagined the regime would have been designed to subdue all individuals into working for a common cause. They would have become closer to each other than anyone could imagine, and would have found that the key to forming a true friendship is to share the same fear of the unknown and be exposed to a common enemy, thereby forming a unique bond never to be found elsewhere. We left for home, but little did we know that a few months later, at the end of our expedition, we would uncannily find ourselves back in the Rose Garden!

OUR TRAINING SESSIONS

Conscientiously, we took many day long trips around the islands of Poole Harbour, going gently at first and gradually becoming more and more adventurous. At first it seemed to take us ages to get anywhere; predictably we went round and round in circles unsteadily until we managed to coordinate our paddle strokes. Eventually, through trial and error, we managed to work out how to turn the canoe quickly, stop, and reverse out of a dangerous situation. The process was sometimes hilarious and gave onlookers from the shore a great deal of amusement, but with perseverance we achieved the correct paddle synchronisation and found ourselves working perfectly in tandem, well-balanced and looking very slick. It wasn't long before we were moving more swiftly, not because of gaining physical strength, but due to our new acquisition of a more skilful and subtle technique. We were soon achieving ten to fifteen miles along the Wareham River, or around Old Harry Rocks to Swanage, at times in some turbulent high seas. We dodged the Sandbanks Ferry by a hair's breadth, ran aground scratching our bottom on the mud banks, and bounced off most of the Harbour islands and surrounding coastline. One Bank Holiday weekend, a simple three or four mile canoe trip in the Sardine to Studland turned into a nightmarish couple of hours. We were pounded and soaked by the wash of what appeared to be at least ten million Bank Holiday pleasure craft, including those infernal jet skies. Frantically, and simultaneously, they barged their way out through the narrow entrance of Poole Harbour. Any consideration to speed limits, or other more vulnerable minute craft such as ours, was nonexistent. Hordes of roaring vessels, spewing out choking exhaust fumes and oily pollution, weaved and hurtled mindlessly through the water at a frightening rate of knots in all directions. Turbulent conditions were created from the wake of all these pleasure boats, leaving us swamped and fighting with our paddles to stay on course and ultimately upright. To these people, navigation and boating etiquette went straight out of the porthole. With glazed eyes, oblivious to anything, including the ferry or any other large shipping, it was full throttle out into the bay and 'look at us in our powerful flashy boat!' A couple of times during our dilemma, Sandra blew her whistle to draw the attention of speeding craft bearing down on us. Infuriatingly, instead of politely and considerately slowing down for us, they just sped past, completely ignoring our plight and looking back with arrogant and ignorant contempt, as we were dangerously tossed around in the wash. From then on, manoeuvres were definitely confined to quiet week days.

OUR CLOTHING

When we began our training sessions it was late winter, very damp and nippy, so warm clothes were an important feature. To save on the commodity that we had little of – money - experiments in dress and glove adaptation were made. All kinds of attire, gloves and hats were tested, including some bizarre items such as yellow washing-up gloves, red rubber gardening gloves, thermal underwear, jackets, and leggings. In the end we resigned to buying wetsuit gloves and footwear, and a set of shower proof jackets and trousers from the outdoor shop. Even 'though it was a summer period when we undertook our trip, we were nevertheless glad of these winter items on the occasional inclement day or chilly evening.

OPERATION FRANKTON CLOTHING

The clothing worn by the men who took part in Operation Frankton, compared to modern day standards, with the advancement and availability of new thermal and gortex substances, was very different to those of today. From our research it would appear that they were issued with the best for the time and that it served them adequately. We believe that people of that era were a lot tougher and hardier than they are now in our pampered, centrally heated, conveyance dominated, sedentary lives. What we now consider to be rough going, to them would be slightly irritating, and what to us would be certain death conditions, they would simply describe as hard going. Having said that, I would not underestimate how savagely cold and uncomfortable it must have been for them, and what terrific psychological pressure they must have had to endure. For 1942, the Cockleshell Heroes wore the latest in combat attire. Each individual boasted one pair of silk gloves covered by a pair of blue woollen mittens. Their legs were adorned with a pair of 'elegant' long woollen underpants, woollen socks, khaki battledress trousers and sea boots. A pair of 'stylish' regulation issue plimsoles was worn under thigh length waders. On top, they wore a woollen under-vest and itchy battledress shirt, covered by a roll neck sweater with a blue scarf wrapped around the neck. Over that lot, they pulled waterproof, mottled olive green camouflaged leggings and a combat smock with a hood that could be pulled up for weather protection or for extra concealment. The smock was fitted with an elasticated skirt that could be attached to the cockpit of the canoe, providing an almost watertight seal from waves washing over the deck. Perched on their heads was a snazzy, dark blue woollen balaclava. It occurred to us, and myself in particular, having personally worn this type of clothing whilst in the Infantry in some very wet and cold conditions, that once all that furry battledress and woollen clothing was saturated, it would have been virtually impossible to dry out during the winter and whilst hiding from the enemy. Worst of all, sitting in a canoe for days on end in those sodden clothes would have been extremely miserable. Beneath the smock was an inflatable life-vest. Each man carried small arms weapons, a Colt 45 automatic pistol and a fighting knife. The unit also carried hand grenades and two silent designed sten guns between them. The sten guns were held by Major Hasler and Lieutenant Mackkinnon.

WATERTIGHT ACCESSORIES

Accessories needed waterproof containers, and so we frugally adapted many things to suit our personal dry needs. The four foot long garden chair covers, that doubled as luxurious 'Sardine' seat cushions and comfortable camp bed mattresses, were sealed inside large green, B&Q, heavy-duty garden refuge bags, and secured together with waterproof duck tape. I bought two waterproof map cases; in one I put the chart, and in the other, my passport, driving paperwork, car keys, telephone numbers, log book and any other important perishable documentation. The waterproof case containing the chart dangled around my neck from the green nylon cord, and the one containing my documents was safely strapped on top of our plastic equipment box situated between my legs. My wallet was in the zip pocket of either my shorts or trousers and wrapped in a double layer of small polythene sandwich bags that I had requisitioned from the kitchen at home. Sandra, whilst browsing in 'Super Buys', discovered a transparent doll sized backpack with zip compartments fitted with a long strap suitable for securing around her neck. She filled the bag with her passport, ferry tickets, euros, mini French dictionary, pen and notebook, etc. Each item was individually wrapped in a sandwich bag, and more vulnerable articles inside a plastic pencil case for double security. This plastic backpack was held squashed between her life-jacket and chest causing some discomfort. However, it was gratifying to know we could be identified if found washed up on the river bank. Our walking boots, socks, sandals, change of clothes, underwear, small backpack, towels, washing and shaving kit, sleeping bags, toolkit, and anything that needed to remain dry, was bundled into double, or treble layers of good old serviceable black bin bags. These proved to be most effective waterproof holding containers, and having a spare roll of fifty of them on board, were so economical and easy to replace if torn.

As well as being watertight, it may seem that our Scrooge-like economies were 'fist-tight'! ..... but semi-retirement, coupled with a passion to travel and extensively explore the planet before infirmity, dictates resourcefulness, creativity, and tight purse strings.

PHYSICAL FITNESS, NAVIGATION AND STAYING AFLOAT

Photograph: Map case and chart

With regard to any extra physical or navigational training, we felt obliged to do something, even 'though we weren't quite sure what! We deliberated over two possibilities: should we book into a gym and start pumping iron, or sign up for seamanship lessons? Neither of us fancied either of those two options. There had to be a compromise between education for the sake of it, and too much exercise that would simply wear us out before we had even started. So we thought fit, walked the mile or so to the local chandlers, and bought a chart of the Gironde River. Later that day, I downloaded a Gironde tide chart from the internet, covering the period of our trip. The printer spat out four or five pieces of A4 that were covered in graphs, names and numbers. Sandra perused over them for a moment, and quickly observed that the river was split into individually named sections, and from that system we could simply calibrate the tide movement by identifying the named segment of the tide chart that we were passing through, by matching it with the area on the sea chart. It sounded complicated ….. she assured me that it was not, but at a glance, the chart looked even more so. My brain cell went into malfunction and Sandra kindly elected to be duty 'tide chart person'. On the following day, the chandlers burnt to the ground. Not sure what the implications of that were but it had two effects: eliminating our exercise, and preventing us wasting any more money on navigational equipment. We had pondered many times in the chandlers over the masses of mind-boggling boating accessories, equipment and fittings. There were compasses, ropes of all colours and gauges (and lengths!), flags representing the letters of the alphabet (didn't Lord Nelson do something with them? ..... "England expects"), miniature kitchen units (yes, I know it's the galley), toilets (heads) with foot pumping flushes, waterproof paint and varnish, sealant, brass ship's bells with 'Titanic' humorously embossed on them, and expensively trendy, but ostensibly functional boating clothes and shoes. Characteristically as canoe owners, we left with nothing more than a packet of Fisherman's Friends. Distress flairs had been considered but they were very expensive, and so we bought two whistles with nylon lanyards, and attached them to our respective life-jackets. On closer scrutiny of the labels, and according to the manufacturer, they are not 'life-jackets' but merely buoyancy aids, and not to be treated as life-saving devices. In smaller print, they also offered the extra reassurance that, in the unlikely event we drowned whilst wearing them, they relinquished all responsibility. Reassuring stuff, but we didn't care what the label said and felt confidently comfortable in them. Our 'buoyancy aids' are quite bulky, colourful, and full of buoyant polystyrene, unlike those flashy little models that hang around the neck like a stole and automatically inflate as soon as one hits the water, sending out a signal to the nearest ship or coastguard. Again they reflected our tight budget.

OUR BUDGET

To call it a budget would be a complete misnomer. As far as our available cash flow was concerned, none was availing itself, and there wasn't any flowing. One problem was that we had already booked a trip to Portugal to attend a family wedding. Coupled with unexpected domestic and vehicle maintenance expenditure, it meant that we had used up most of our surplus funds. After a short debate, Sandra and I came up with the obvious answer ..... sponsorship! It was decided that we should embark upon a fund raising exercise. Neither of us had a clue what to do, who to approach, or where we should begin. What we did know, however, was that if nothing else, it was imperative that we secure the price of our ferry ticket, our largest financial item. If we didn't, we weren't going anywhere, and that was for certain. As we were an unknown quantity, it was obvious to us that we needed to legitimise the expedition and give it kudos. It was imperative that we present any potential sponsors with evidence, an image of confidence, and reassurance that we were both determined and one hundred percent genuine. What our project needed was some kind of endorsement or support from an independent party. The ingredient that we desperately required was something that said, "This event really is going to happen." One of the essential missing links to validate our expedition was publicity, newsworthiness and press coverage. Something not in our favour, however, was that we were not doing it for charity, but we both knew that to raise sponsorship, we had to stimulate some tangible, marketable interest.

PUBLICITY
THE LOCAL ECHO AND THE BBC TV NEWS

A 'phone call to the News Desk at the Bournemouth Daily Echo found us in conversation with the columnist and reporter Diana Henderson. As a skilled interviewer and reporter, Diana immediately put us at our ease, making conversation with her most relaxed and informal. Uninhibited by her communicative manner, we were gushing fluent with our proposed plans and ideas. All the while she displayed a genuine interest and enthusiasm for the topic. Finally, she asked us to email her an outline/synopsis of our trip, including some of the background and history of the Cockleshell Heroes. On receipt of the same, and once she had read it, Diana was soon calling us back to see if we possessed any suitable photographs to accompany her proposed newspaper feature. Once she had downloaded and surveyed the two 'naff' amateur pictures that I had attached to an email, a photo shoot with professional photographers was arranged. Filled with excitement, we prepared ourselves. It was agreed, over copious cups of tea (our solution to any impending or current dilemma), that most important was our image. The only obstacle that we could envisage at that stage was that we didn't have an image. It wasn't going to look very adventurous or impressive in the newspaper photograph to see us both paddling gently along the Sandbanks shoreline on a tranquil sunny day, simply dressed in shorts and tee shirts. To summon up interest and procure sponsorship, we needed to project something more gritty and dramatic. Drama was going to be difficult to produce at short notice, especially in a still photograph, so the least we could do was to look the part. The theme of our trip being military, I retired to the garden shed, and from a high dusty shelf amongst the slug pellets and cracked flower pots, I pulled down a large cardboard box containing my dubiously acquisitioned, long since discarded Army clothing from my service with the Infantry. After a short hilarious fancy dress routine, two camouflaged combat caps were selected and placed jauntily upon our heads. Mine was a good fit but Sandra, having a voluminous head of voluptuous bouncy hair, required the extra security of two large hair grips. Dressed to kill in our combat caps, dark green waterproof jackets and matching leggings, we now both certainly looked the business. The Cockleshell Heroes would have been proud of us.

PHOTO SHOOT

On a grey, wet and windy day, utilising the stony slipway adjacent to the East Dorset Sailing Club, we slid the Sardine over the small rocks and pebbles and into Poole Harbour, whilst the Echo photographer and her assistant snapped away from the shore. She lent, bent, knelt, twisted and crawled over the rocky shore, adopting almost every conceivable and seemingly excruciatingly uncomfortable posture and angle imaginable to achieve the desired effect. It must be said that it was all well worth the effort, and much to her professionalism and credit, she produced a most flattering and dynamic photograph. This picture, along with a well constructed article (I did the initial draft which was then skilfully edited by Diana), subsequently appeared in the Daily Echo. Our next port of call was the BBC TV station. An email from us to the BBC with attached photograph received a positive response with the promise of documentation on the regional news programme. The effect on us was more euphoria, dancing round the room with flutes of bubbly. At last we had something tangible, the ball really was rolling; now all we required was a sponsorship covering letter.

SPONSORSHIP

Out came the laptop, and after some profound thought and deliberation over the content, like which tack to use - straight forward, begging, or subtle manipulation - a well rounded letter was composed. Duplicates of the covering letter with boastful mention of possible BBC TV coverage, along with copies of the newspaper feature bearing our photograph, were hastily produced on the local ironmonger's five pence a time photocopy machine, and thrust expectantly in envelopes. Our targets were canoe and boating equipment manufacturers, and the ferry company. Addresses written, stamps applied and fingers crossed, our mail shot went straight into the post box. Days of the usual junk mail and bills went by, followed by weeks that were followed by disillusionment. Whilst mulling over our predicament, it once again became obvious to us that one of our expedition's negative and unattractive points, even 'though we had the news coverage, was that we were not supporting a charity. As the trip was a tribute, combined with personal adventure, collecting for charity was not relevant to this scenario. Eventually two replies miraculously arrived on the same day - one from the canoe manufacture who kindly sent us a few items for a raffle ..... two large baseball caps, a medium sized vacuum flask, and a small sweatshirt bearing the company logo. The other, more official letter from Brittany Ferries, offered us a substantial reduction off our tickets. Whoopee! Yes, we were now definitely going.

BBC TV NEWS SHOOT

A few days later on a bright sunny morning, we packed all our expedition equipment and belongings into the car and hauled the Sardine on to the roof rack. We were scheduled to meet the BBC TV team at the same spot as the photo shoot, on the harbour shoreline at 10am. At one minute to ten, the mobile rang, and the reporter, Richard Drax, informed us that it was off! A bleak moment of depression swept over us. Apparently there had been some new developments regarding a local murder, and as he was the only reporter in this area, he had to cover the story. A new date in two days time was set. The irritating thing was that they hadn't even found the murderer or murderess, just a microscopic piece of evidence. Obviously the murder was more newsworthy than two people about to set off on a death defying trip. Having psyched ourselves up into a frenzy of anticipation, it was doubly disappointing and a nuisance because we had told many friends that we would be on the evening news, plus the fact that we had risen early and had packed everything ready to go. Another worrying point was that for the last week or so the weather had been fine and settled, but the evening before, the weather forecasters were grimly predicting a big change. There were a lot of arrows and grim, swirly, graphicy stuff across the TV weather map. Sure enough the rearranged date had to be cancelled because of stormy weather. We didn't hear from the BBC again and felt rather deflated, having assumed that they had gone off the boil with regard to our story. About a week before the trip, I emailed the News Desk. Then a reply came back with an apology for not being in touch, and the shoot was rescheduled ….. the TV were on their way to meet us in Poole! Even 'though we had worked as actors and supporting artists on hundreds of film and TV sets in the past, this film shoot was great fun for us and our inflated egos, as we were the main attraction. Richard Drax and his one- man crew were both easy going and approachable chaps. They knew what they wanted, and we willingly obeyed their direction. Coincidentally, a pile of empty cockleshells had been discarded by fisherman on our 'launching pad' which seemed a good omen and appropriate place to start filming. Then followed some shots of all our gear and the chart spread out on the rocky shore against and over the Sardine. The cameraman reset his tripod and camera apparatus precariously on the top of a large bolder made slippery by seaweed. From this vantage point near the water's edge, he filmed us boarding the Sardine, launching ourselves without falling in. All the time we were conscious that we should look as professional and wobble free as possible. There was one dodgy moment when I discovered that I had absentmindedly left my paddle on shore. My solution was to stand up and twist round to retrieve it which caused an anxious moment in the choppy waves. Having a good sense of balance, I managed to recover my composure. In addition to the BBC, we had invited two photographer friends along to capture the scene with some still pictures. They voiced their disappointment that I had not given them a gratuitous shot of me plunging undignified into the water. With the BBC cameraman sprawled prone across the pebbles just inches from the rippling waves, we followed his instruction and paddled madly away from the shore until we heard his voice, faint over the wind and wave noise, requesting us to paddle swiftly back towards him. He followed that sequence by requesting us to paddle parallel to the shore, first in one direction and then the other. A small amphibious camera was then attached to the rear of the canoe for a close-up action image. Having taken enough paddling footage in that location, we came ashore for the interview. Richard Drax was light-hearted and his questions were predictable and to the point, "Why were we doing it, what was our inspiration and the background of the original Operation?"

Following the interview, we swiftly packed up and relocated to Poole Quay where, as members of British Actors' Equity, our acting skills came into their own. With the camera rolling, we paddled dramatically alongside a very conveniently moored and most befitting German tanker, and pretended to affix limpet mines against its hull. Action complete, we pulled away and headed back towards the quay where throngs of inquisitive people had crowded around the camera.

Over a post shoot drink at 'The Jolly Sailor', the BBC chaps suggested that we contact the local French TV or some dignitary, like the Mayor of Bordeaux, but we were reluctant. The BBC news coverage and local publicity were quite enough to make it feel special to us, our friends, the viewers, and the local community. Imagine the responsibility that would have been resting on our shoulders if some kind of welcoming reception had been organised by the Mayor of Bordeaux! He or she could have been standing there on a rostrum at the edge of the quay with the TV news cameras poised for a shot of our arrival, everyone gazing down the rushing River Gironde, but no sign of us. We could have sunk halfway, or our canoe could have been stolen as we slept in our tent on the river bank. Paranoia such as that prevented us from arranging receptions or 'doing it for charity'.

Two days later, a call from the BBC informed us that our piece would be shown that evening. Ensconced in our seats in front of the TV, finger primed over the video record button of the remote control, we waited with bated breath, enduring all the previous items until, yes!, there we were, on the telly. The comprehensive broadcast was very impressive, with an informative preamble outlining the actual mission.

TRANSCRIPT OF BBC TV INTERVIEW

RICHARD: "This mission won't be quite so hazardous, as the couple are the first to admit."

ROGER: "Obviously we won't be threatened by the enemy, or anything like that ..... our only enemy will be having to drink wine and eat cheese in France!"

SANDRA: "Of course, we're going in July, when obviously it's going to be better weather ..... they went in December, but even so, it's going to be a bit tough, I think."

RICHARD: "The couple have been training hard, and here in Poole Harbour they got just a little taste of how vulnerable those men must have felt as they went from ship to ship placing their explosive charges."

ROGER: "They had ammunition and weapons .....

SANDRA: "And the limpet mines .....

ROGER: "And the limpet mines, and all that kind of stuff, so they were really well laden. But with all the gear in, it is ballast; it does make it nice and comfortable to ride."

SANDRA: "My friends think I'm mad that I can spend ten days living out of a little bag, but I'm going to enjoy it."

ROGER: "We can only last ten days because her make-up will run out!"

RICHARD: "No explosions this time 'though, just there own personal tribute to a special group of men ..... Richard Drax, for BBC South Today."

The feature went on to give a good pictorial and graphic account of our potential escapade. The edited shots of us crossing the harbour and surreptitiously approaching the tanker were shown in grainy black and white, giving it that authentic, sinister look ..... admirable. We were surprised by how many people had seen us and were interested to hear an update. People we had never seen before would stop us and say, "Did you do it?" "How did it go?" and "Are you going to write a book about it?"

BBC RADIO

A spin off from the BBC TV interest was that we received a call from BBC Radio Solent. The girl asked if I would take part in a telephone interview. I agreed and she said that she would ring off, go to the correct studio, and call me back in a few minutes. As promised, she called back and instructed me to speak into the 'phone whilst she carried out a sound check to achieve a level on her recording equipment. "Testing, testing, one two, one two," I eloquently orated down the telephone handset, in true roady lingo. "Ok, I'm switching it on now," she warned. This had the immediate effect of putting me on edge. The questions, as with the TV, were pretty puerile and predictable, and I replied with my set pieces outlining our inspiration and some brief background to Operation Frankton. She prompted me into a request for sponsorship which was useful, so I confirmed that we were on the look out for any philanthropic persons who liked the sound of our venture, but then suddenly she changed tack and interjected with, "How do you think your adventure will benefit the people of Poole?" Her question was unnerving and I found it difficult to come up with an instant logical answer. I thought it was a stupid thing to ask and decided right or wrong to be frank and say whatever came into my head. "It won't," I replied. "It won't benefit them at all. It's just pure self-indulgence, a personal challenge for our own gratification, but most of all our tribute to the Cockleshell Heroes." After that the interview fizzled out and she thanked me for taking part. Not having the time to listen to BBC Radio Solent all day, we had no idea whether or not it had been transmitted. Eventually, through an acquaintance, we discovered that it had indeed been broadcast. No sponsorship materialised as a result.

STOWING OUR EQUIPMENT

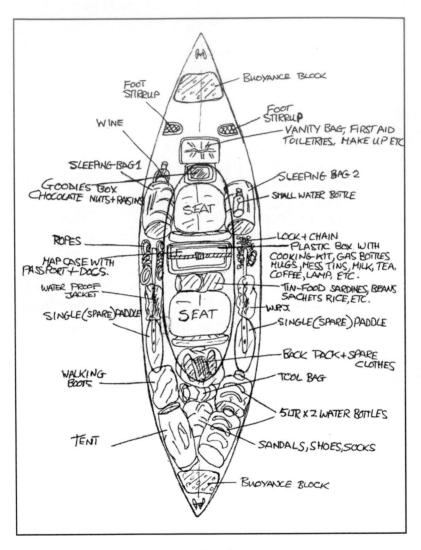

Illustration: 'Sardine' contents

Before actually launching the Sardine fully laden, Sandra and I decided (to save any embarrassing sinking in public episodes) that we would sit the Sardine on the green grass of our back lawn and there we would stuff it, or nautically speaking, stow it with all our accoutrements. Even 'though we were going to be roughing it, we were determined to make things as comfortable as possible in such confined and restricted conditions. I was conscious of my Infantry training. 'Fit to Fight' was the motto that the Special Forces' instructors constantly drummed into us. "Save your heroics for the battlefield. You're no use to anyone if you arrive to engage the enemy worn out, starving and suffering from hypothermia. Take the most direct, least strenuous but tactical route, eat as well as resources can supply, and sleep as warm, dry and comfortable as you can. You will then be fit to fight." Fifty minutes or more of nerve fraying, sweat inducing, knuckle grazing trial and error were endured. Things were nicely folded, and if they didn't fit, taken out and then rolled, and then if they still refused to fit, they were just squashed in with brute force and ignorance. To the left and right of Sandra's bow seat lay our sleeping bags. Between leg space, and slightly forward under the foredeck, was a medium sized, 'salmon pink', canvas, zip top vanity holdall. Contents top secret. On top of that sat a plastic container of light refreshments ..... Kendall's mint cake, chocolate nuts and raisins, and pistachio nuts. Amidships, between my legs, strapped to the hull frame (on the bailing sponge), was a large plastic box containing the cooking stove, matches, mess tins, spare gas cylinders, gas lamp and spare mantles, canoe repair kit, tape, spare tent pegs, sachets of dried food, tea, coffee, powered milk, Horlicks, vitamin supplements, plastic knives, forks, spoons, plates, mugs and wine goblets, washing-up items, insect repellent burning sticks, and dried instant mash potato. Directly behind that in a bin liner was our tinned and packet food, i.e. veggie sausage and beans all-day-breakfast, sardines, instant flavoured rice, black pepper, ship's biscuits, plus toilet roll, etc. By my feet, and either side of my seat, were the spare set of single paddles, garden trowel (toilets for the use of), shower proof hooded jackets and leggings, mooring ropes, first aid box, camera, chains, and locks. Housed aft, and directly behind my seat, was the backpack containing spare clothes and washing and shaving kit. Behind that were the tool bag and sack containing sandals and socks. The starboard aft housed two five litre water bottles, and down the port side we stored the tent and sack with walking boots. It might not sound much to the normal holiday maker with a 22 kilo suitcase allowance, but in the Sardine, believe me, it was the limit.

Stuffing complete, we then squeezed ourselves in amongst it all. Gripping the sides with our hands, we lowered ourselves in – Sandra forward, with me, aft - and with a little ungainly, delicate manoeuvring of our legs and stern ends, plop! ..... we were in. Although it was compact and we were squashed in like (our namesake) sardines, it was surprisingly comfortable. This was because we had our four foot long camping mattresses on our seats. It meant that instead of our legs lying straight ahead and directly on the hull, we were resting them on the length of our mattresses. Sandra positioned her feet on two grooved stirrups that were located on each side of the forward bulkhead, whilst my feet were simply placed either side of her upright seat back. When we attached the canvas spray deck, we realised Sandra's long legs might be a problem. Increased by the extra height of the mattress and surrounding packages, her knees stuck up forming bulges in the canvas. Although the stirrups were adjustable, she preferred not to have them too far away as she felt she needed to push against them to maximise the momentum of her paddling. Pinned in tight with so much equipment, we became blatantly aware of the one most important safety aspect ..... it was glaringly obvious, even on the lawn, that not only should we be able to get in the Sardine, but in a capsize situation, we must be able to get out, and quickly! Sandra, sitting at the front with her legs under the foredeck, had to arrange all the front clobber in such a way as to afford her adequate emergency exit room. I, on the other hand, would hopefully find it slightly easier, in theory, to extricate myself. Subsequently, I drew a contents sketch plan to remember where everything went.

COCKLESHELL HEROES EQUIPMENT

Although we considered the Sardine to be packed tight and heavy, our overall weight compared to the canoes used on the actual Operation was relatively light. Besides all their personal weapons, fighting knives, pistols, sten guns, and hand grenades, they had their ration packs, water, survival gear, and escape bags for after the Operation, plus the most important items of all, the high explosive limpet mines - eight per canoe, each weighing ten pounds. The limpet mines were designed to clamp magnetically on to the side of a ship, six feet below the waterline. Each limpet mine contained 4 kilos of explosive and was fitted with a fizzing, preset timed fuse that would ultimately blow a whopping great hole in the side of the enemy ship. The technique they practised over and over again was as follows: each canoe would float silently alongside the target ships, and whilst one man using a strong magnetic 'holdfast' device kept the canoe in position, the other man would lower the limpet mine, attached to a six foot placing rod, below the water, and clamp it to the hull of the ship.

OUR ROUTE

It was important to us that our route was the same as, or as close as possible to, that taken by the Cockleshell Heroes. For us to be denied any part of it would have been more than just disappointing.

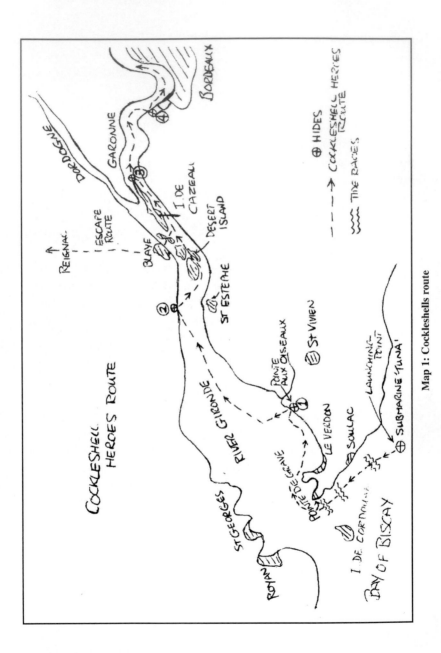

Map 1: Cockleshells route

COCKLESHELLS ROUTE

The members of Operation Frankton began their long journey from England to the start point, a grid reference in the Bay of Biscay, some ten miles southward from the headland called Pointe de Grave at the entrance to the River Gironde, in the care of a submarine named 'Tuna' (registered in Gosport). The voyage took them five hot, claustrophobic days, dramatically highlighted by a terrifying, mind concentrating depth charge attack, perpetrated by a German war ship. They clung on, teeth clenched, enduring the fearsome underwater buffeting for minutes that seemed like hours until the enemy lost contact, or simply gave up. During the beginning of their trip, they were all (apart from Major Hasler and the submarine captain, for security sensitivity) under the erroneous impression that it was just another exercise. That idea was soon to be erased. Once submerged and into their underwater cruise, Major Hasler called his men together in a small space near the torpedo area. On a blackboard, he drew an outline of the Gironde estuary, and revealed to them the true reason for their presence in the confines of this tin fish. They were all relieved to discover that at last, after so many months of gruelling training, they were now about to put their new hard-earned skills into action, but most importantly, get a crack at the enemy. This was a major motivation to many, in particular Bill Sparks who had lost his brother in a naval engagement with the Germans. The Cockleshells were launched from the 'Tuna' on to an oily calm sea, but it was not to be without snags. The procedure of manhandling them from below decks on to the open deck of the submarine was a delicate one, and unfortunately the flimsy canvas of 'Cachalot' was severely torn on a rough hatch clamp on its way up. Major Hasler was forced to make a quick assessment and his decision was, 'I'm afraid it can't go'. This was a soul-destroying moment for the two crew members, Ellery and Fisher, and quite understandably they were devastated. After all they had gone through in training, they were now to return with the 'Tuna'. Mortified, Fisher broke down on the spot and sobbed.

OUR ROUTE (continued)

Photograph: Departure, Brittany Ferry, Poole Harbour.

Not having the facility of a submarine or any form of support vessel, our journey began from Poole Harbour, using our concessionary tickets on the 7.30am Brittany Condor Ferry. Having spent a smooth crossing downing copious bottomless cups of free refills of coffee, we arrived, wide-eyed with caffeine, two hours later in Cherbourg. The AA route that we had requested seemed too complicated to follow, and in one instance, inaccurate. Their suggestion that we 'join the toll free motorway' turned out to be incorrect and cost us a bunch of euros! After 350 miles, and infinite rolling fields of big yellow sunflowers that gently swayed and smiled at us, we arrived at our destination, the large bay of St Georges de Didonne. With the help of a jolly, animated family who managed to understand Sandra's rusty French, we were directed from the little port, up the well worn stone steps by the lighthouse, and along the narrow path at the top of the cliff towards the Cockleshell Heroes Memorial which had been unveiled by Bill Sparks on the 50th anniversary of Operation Frankton. It was a curvaceous, contemporary styled sculpture with an inscription to the memory of the men and their task, and our first evidence and confirmation that we were now on the right track. Stretching out before us, as the wind tried to tear our hair from its roots, was the vast Gironde estuary .... daunting, rough, windy and bleak .....

Photograph: Cockleshell Heroes Memorial, St Georges de Didonne

we were speechless! It took forty five minutes of pitching and rolling on the last ferry from Royan (twinned with Gosport) to cross the estuary to Pointe de Grave on the west bank. On the way, having left our vehicle on the car deck, we climbed the iron steps to the inappropriately named sun deck, and absorbed the stimulating, sea spray saturated wind. Some German tourists were fascinated by our canoe perched on top of the car, and seeing the sea state, were surprised to hear that we were going to be taking it on the river. Conversation with them concerning our adventure was selectively discreet, and we adopted the policy of 'don't mention the war' with regard to the true theme. Back on terrafirma, we drove our Mondeo Estate, with the Sardine proudly attached to the roof rack, up the bumpy ramp, out of the terminal at Pointe de Grave, and along the narrow, silver sand lined bendy road towards Soulac. Obviously, without a support boat, it was impossible for us to start our journey exactly where the Cockleshell Heroes had begun theirs, at a grid reference ten miles out in the Bay of Biscay. Therefore, as a compromise, we decided to start from Soulac, a small seaside town, situated south, just along the sandy shoreline from the entrance to the River Gironde. Soulac is now a bustling, respectable touristy town, with a thriving high street boasting lots of cafés, restaurants and bars, with marvellously vibrant and garish street entertainment. During our evening reccie of Soulac, we were entertained by an ostentatiously dressed, flamboyant French Elvis who pranced and crooned in a red sequined, high collared jacket, from a rickety, makeshift stage to an enthralled and amused audience. Continuing our gentle perambulation further along the bustling precinct, we came across some nubile, scantily clad female carnival dancers, cavorting through the happy throng. Their licentiously provocative gyrations were accompanied by two animated male drummers. It was a clear dry night, made cold by a bitter wind from the sea. Leaving the buzz and lights of the town behind us, we wandered hand-in-hand down the dark, windy beach to the shoreline. With the waves rolling in and the wind biting the skin on our exposed faces, we gazed silently out into the dark, murky sea, reflecting on how terrible it must have been for those men out there on that December night in 1942. In the darkness to our right, we could just pick out the shape of the Island of Cordouan with its giant lighthouse. The Cockleshell Heroes had to navigate unseen between this and the other lighthouse on the mainland opposite at Pointe de Grave. With its 25,000 candle power lamp sweeping across the estuary, they must have suffered some nail biting minutes ..... a thought provoking and very humbling start to our journey ..... we hoped that we could do them justice.

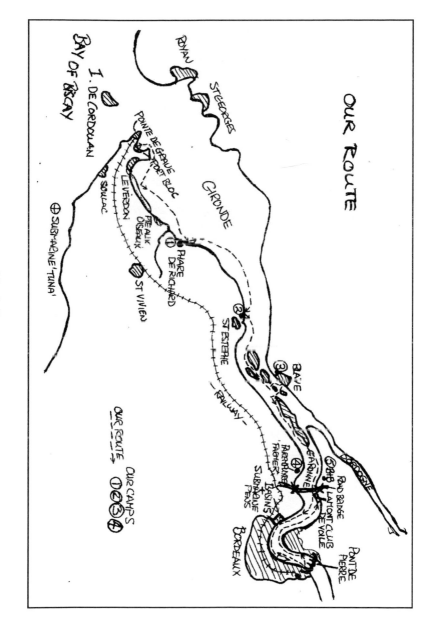

Map 2: Our route

'SARDINE' ITINERARY
Expedition date 12th – 21st July 2004

Car Ferry from Poole Harbour to France, drive to Soulac.
Reccie coast area for launching location.
Locate bus station. Check return times etc.

Estimated travel distance in canoe, 15-20 sea miles per day.
Estimated sailing time from Soulac to Bordeaux, 6-7 days.

Route and suggested stops

Day 1. Leave *Soulac*, follow coastline to Pointe de Grave.
Continue into River Gironde as far as *Le Verdon*. First camp.

Day 2. From *Le Verdon*, second leg to *Pointe aux Oiseaux*.
Second camp.

Day 3. From *Pointe aux Oiseaux*, paddle across river and find
rough area of 2nd Cockleshell night hide and stopover. Find
suitable camp location or site. If no suitable site found, cross river
to St Estephe and find accommodation area.

Day 4. Cross river, or leave *St Estephe* and reccie the various
islands lying in the centre of the river, including the '*Desert
Island*'. Cross river to *Blaye* for the night.

Day 5. Back across to *Margeaux* or further to Cockleshell stop 3
area.

Day 6. Last leg on the Garonne to Pontoon Pier and Bordeaux
Docks. Bread, Cheese and Wine party. Check museums and
memorials. Find campsite or accommodation and bus location.
Secure canoe.

Day 7. Return by bus to *Soulac*, retrieve car, return to *Bordeaux*,
collect canoe and begin return journey to *England*. Mission
completed.

This is a tight but quite feasible schedule, and therefore there is a
flexible contingency of three extra days built into the project.

PADDLING THE COURSE

THE START POINT: Monday 12th July

Following our reccie of Soulac and the Bay of Biscay coastline, we had reluctantly but unanimously decided (following a heated debate between Sandra and me on the ferry crossing from Royan to Pointe de Grave, via the turbulent waters at the mouth of the Gironde) that because of the rough sea conditions and strong wind, a launch from the coastline beach into crashing waves was just too hazardous for our heavily laden canoe. My initial stubborn instinct had been to press on with a launch from the beach at Soulac and into the sea as planned, whatever the conditions. However, Sandra was quite uneasy and made her point most vehemently. With her words still ringing in my ears, I returned to the dark and eerie beach to have one more look at the sea state. The wind was strong, in the wrong direction, and the waves crashing on to the shore were far too high for our low profile craft. Logically, it didn't seem that things on that stretch of coast would change dramatically by the morning either. I returned to the car and conceded to Sandra that, yes, we might make it, but it seemed pointless for us to take the risk of getting swamped before we had even started, and without the aid of a support boat, it would be just too foolhardy. Therefore plan 'B' swung into action, and we settled for our alternative start point choice, the ferry terminal and marina area of Port Bloc, adjacent to Pointe de Grave. Leaving Soulac, we drove back to the estuary and pitched our estate car in the ferry terminal car park, drew the makeshift curtains (attached by string across the windows), and enjoyed a sound, comfortable (thanks to a mattress from home), undisturbed night's sleep.

DAY ONE: Tuesday 13th July

As first light filtered through the curtains about 6.45am, we wiped the condensation from the windows, unlocked the door, crept bright-eyed out of the car, and found that it was a lot colder than we had anticipated, and so we slipped on our jackets. Within fifty metres of the ferry terminal car park, we discovered a diminutive sandy bay which formed part of the Port Bloc harbour and marina. Situated conveniently at the top of the beach, above the spot where we decided to launch the Sardine, stood a typically French, immodestly constructed very public toilet block. It was basic but serviceable and fulfilled our third class morning ablution requirements. Conscious that it would be a day or two before we would enjoy such a facility, I gave my teeth a jolly good brushing, leaving just enough enamel to ward off wine and cheese rot. I had my electric shaver with at least thirty minutes battery time, so there was no danger off me growing a designer sailor's beard. Having unloaded the Sardine from our roof rack, set it on the sandy shore with all the gear installed, we lit the single Calor gas burner and set about a quick breakfast of baked beans and veggie sausages, all washed down with large, black, army issue mugs of hot tea. As we sat hunched and silent in thoughtful contemplation, clutching our mugs to warm our fingers, we stared down at the Sardine, alone at the edge of the water, loaded and ready for action. The paddles were lying beside it on the sand, ready to be taken up. There was an air of anticipation that something dynamic was about to happen. The scene was motionless but primed. After breakfast, we were disconcertingly approached by a smart English vagrant with a bike and small backpack. The man had a suspicious manner that made us feel uneasy and cautious. He was trying to cadge a cigarette and a euro towards a ferry ticket over to Royan. Having refused his rather aggressive, possibly drink fuelled demands, he left us alone and wandered off wheeling his bike, looking a little disgruntled to try it on with some other people near the terminal. This incident left us a slightly concerned with regard to the safety of our vehicle whilst we were away. It was obvious from the contents of our canoe that we were going for some time.

Therefore, the thought of him stealing it, or even breaking in and sleeping in it, did momentarily pass through our consciousness. However, leaving the car to its own fate was already planned, so we didn't dwell on the dire possibilities.

AT LAST, WE WERE OFF!!

Having parked the car in the most unsuspicious looking spot in the ferry terminal car park, we dragged the Sardine down to the water's edge. As we squashed into our sturdy vessel, there was the realisation that we had packed more than we had originally intended. There was no excess baggage fee, so no worries, we were afloat! Excitedly, setting our paddles at precisely 9.30am into the calm, brackish water of the Gironde for the first of many thousands of strokes to come, we manoeuvred confidently through the private moorings and small fishing smacks towards the narrow Port Bloc marina entrance. As a reassuringly brilliant start and prime example of our professionalism, we immediately found ourselves blushingly lost amongst the labyrinth of floating pontoons, up a cul-de-sac with rows of moored private boats. Humiliated, imagining that the whole world was aware, even 'though there was hardly anyone around, we made an undignified withdrawal and started again. On our second approach to the port exit, we encountered a huge (compared to us) noisy rust bucket, a sinister looking dredger moving unpredictably backwards and forwards, in and out of the port entrance. Studying the rhythm of its movements as we approached, on its reverse motion, we gripped our paddles and made a dash for the open river, just making it before it began to swing back into the tight gap. At last, we were on our way ..... unfettered, unstoppable and independent. The water was smooth with just a slight ripple, characteristically brown and murky, and the sky overcast with the sun trying to break through. The wind was slight and behind us ..... all together a good start. Ahead and stretching across to our left, as we paddled, lay the massive La Gironde, flowing majestically and disappearing into the far distant haze. A wave of excitement, coupled with a little trepidation, surged through our bodies at the sudden realisation of the challenge ahead of us. It was a weird feeling, setting off into the unknown in our new compact home with all our worldly possessions squeezed in around us. We both expressed our identical sensation at that poignant moment. The Sardine was small, packed with us and all our chattels. From now on, the Sardine and its contents were all that we had, and it was going to be our transport and home for as long as it took to do what we had set out to do. There was no turning back, the river and its mysteries lay before us, we were on our own and underway.

Our minds were quickly brought back to the job in hand when the wretched dredger crept up from behind and passed us, apparently on a course for mid-river, possibly to disgorge its bloated bellyful of mud. Discourteously, it pompously left us rocking violently, having to stabilise ourselves in its formidable wake. After fifteen minutes or so, we arrived at a dilapidated, partially collapsed and crumbling disused concrete pier structure belonging to the area of Le Verdon. Intrusively it jutted a long way out into the river, probably five hundred yards or so. As we passed cautiously under it, we hung on to one of its massive struts for a moment and gazed back at Pointe de Grave. Worryingly Sandra said, "I don't know how I'm going to do this," as the strain of holding the paddle up was already becoming uncomfortable ..... and we'd only just started! The concrete strut was heavily encrusted with oysters. I knocked a couple off with the blade of my paddle and lay them on my canvas deck. In my ignorance, I later fatuously dropped them into the water. This action I later regretted when I bought some in the street market at Blaye, and realised that if only I had opened them, I could have eaten them there and then.

COCKLESHELLS DISASTEROUS BEGINNING

The mission was undertaken during winter when the nights were longest. For obvious tactical reasons, Hasler chose the 'dark period' i.e. four to six days extending either side of the new moon. This also had the advantage of the tides being at 'Springs' and therefore at their highest – full flood – thereby producing the strongest currents to assist acceleration. The downside was that it was also at its lowest ebb, producing long mud banks to negotiate. Although we went during a different season, the phases of the moon were (not by our design but once again by the hand of fate) almost identical, and the spring tides were of a similar ferocity which, although good for our propulsion, made our journey all the more challenging.

It occurred to us that by the time the commandos had reached this area of Le Verdon, it was roughly three o'clock in the morning. They had been paddling for over six hours and had already suffered tragedy when, shortly after leaving the submarine Tuna, they met up with three unpredicted and uncharted tidal races. Two canoes capsized. One disappeared and, unknown to the rest of the party at the time, the two crew members, Sergeant Wallace and Ewart, paddled on nearly all night until they were capsized by rough surf near Pointe de Grave. They managed to swim ashore but were captured, tortured and interrogated. They disclosed nothing and were eventually moved to Bordeaux. In the early hours of the 11th December, just as Hasler and Laver were approaching their targets a mile or so away, Wallace and Ewart were driven to a lonely sandpit in a nearby wood, and tied to two wooden stakes. Two open coffins were placed in front of them to emphasise the point that they were about to be sent to the final RV. Their vulnerable bodies were illuminated by the headlamps of the army lorry that had previously conveyed them, and they were callously shot. The second canoe that capsized, after several fruitless attempts to right it by Bill Sparks, had to be scuttled. The two jettisoned crew, Moffat and Sheard, hung on to Major Hasler and Mackinnons' canoes, treading the freezing sea. Passing the dangerous, enemy occupied area of the port of Le Verdon, the two canoes were labouring desperately under the dead weight of the men they were towing, and it became increasingly difficult to handle them in the fast tide. With much heart wrenching reluctance, Major Hasler, blatantly aware of the vulnerability to his mission, had to leave them to swim for it. The two men by that time had been in the freezing water for over an hour, and were physically weak and suffering terribly from hypothermia. The remainder of the party paddled on, having witnessed two of their close friends drift away into the dark inky night to certain death. Hasler tried to subdue his emotion, but Sparks could hear his commander sobbing. (Long after the Operation it was discovered that Moffat's body and canoe were washed up on the beach at Les Sables d'Olonne, seventy miles away, and Sheard was never heard of again.) Following that, they had to carefully and silently pass three Chasseur type German destroyers anchored in line in preparation for an inspection the next day. Hasler decided they would go one at a time, passing between the destroyers and under a small jetty patrolled by a German sentry. When they came out the other side, they had lost Mackinnon and Conway. They heard a gun shot and raised voices from the jetty area. Had Mackinnon and Conway been shot or captured? They didn't know but understood that nothing must jeopardise the momentum of the Operation, and the two remaining canoes continued on. It would be another three hours before their first stop. (Long after the mission was completed, it was learned that Mackinnon and Conway had continued on courageously alone).

OUR EASY START

The chart, in its waterproof, see-through pouch, hung around my neck from a long piece of green nylon string. The only problem was that after folding it several times to make it fit in, I had put it in the wrong way up. Now, every time I flicked it up to look at it, it was upside-down. A quick release of its Velcro seal, and it was readjusted. Moving on past the giant concrete structure of a deserted container port to our right, we once again found ourselves paddling at top speed to avoid the phantom dredger. Having been to the centre of the river to do whatever it had to do, it had now taken it into its mechanical head to come charging back and moor alongside the empty container quay. Navigation at this early stage was turning out not to be quite as simple as we had first thought. We constantly misjudged our position, and being so low in the water, it was difficult to see landmarks and recognise or pinpoint any obvious sea markers. The coastline was flat, uninspiringly bland, and visually extremely difficult to compare with our chart. In comparison, the opposite east bank in the far distance appeared through the murky visibility to be more picturesque, with undulating green hills and chalky cliffs. It felt comforting to associate them with our own 'White Cliffs of Dover'. So considering the theme of our journey, and with just us and an enormous empty estuary for company, a rough chorus of 'The White Cliffs of Dover', in true Vera Lynne wartime fashion, reverberated over the Gironde. Large, ostensibly visible oyster beds were indicated on the chart, but we couldn't see them either, and it was difficult to negotiate the many sandbanks and rotten wooden protrusions that gave us many false reckonings. The supposedly semi-submerged, but still visible, shipwreck also marked on the chart, which would have given us a positive position, also managed to elude us. Our new strategy, devised out of frustration, became, 'As long as the land was on our right, and we were in the water, not the mud (which was happening all too frequently), we were ok'. Nevertheless, we had our first nautical disagreement as Sandra thought we had kept far too close in to the mudflats, and although enjoying the rare opportunity of observing the many varieties of sea birds at such close quarters, we had travelled much further than necessary in a dogleg. After an hour or so of paddling with a false sense of security, the weather changed. Swells with choppy and quite large running waves over the sandbanks were now the order of the day. We were now also aware of the enormous thrust and power of the tide. This was good for momentum but not for making any misjudgements in balance or direction. Pushing on, paddling a grey and dismal coastline, we heard gunfire ..... at the same stretch where the Heroes had heard it! ..... and found ourselves at Pointe aux Oiseaux. This was the spot where we estimated that the Cockleshell Heroes had made their first stop. Paddles inboard, drifting with the strong current and rocking gently to the Gironde River rhythm, I pulled the camera from under the canvas deck, passed it carefully to Sandra in the front, and she clicked a pictorial record of the historic spot. Whilst resting our arms, we assessed our inept navigational start to the expedition, and marvelled at the Heroes amazing ability to navigate in the pitch dark on that freezing December night. Major Hasler, Bill Sparks, Laver and Mills, we reflected, had arrived at this spot, having paddled for a gruelling, frightening, bitterly cold and wet eleven hours, covering roughly twenty six miles.

OUR FIRST STOP

Photograph: Crusoe Island, Our 1st Camp

It had been our intention to stop at Pointe aux Oiseaux, but as we had made good time, and we were still uncertain of our chances of success, we decided to push on. Thirty minutes paddling later, we passed the well kept, but non-functional, white lighthouse – Le Phare de Richard - its rocky base adorned by a couple of solemn looking, mildly bemused, gnome-like fishermen. We interpreted their frowning facial expressions from beneath their peaked caps as, 'Don't disturb the fish with those paddles, and keep away from our lines'. Another quarter of a mile brought us to a small, grassy tufted peninsular with a sheltered sandy cove. Seeing our rest place for the night, our tiredness quickly subsided, and a sudden surge of latent energy and boost of morale flooded through our veins. One brief, enthusiastic dash of the paddles sent the bows of the Sardine and its relieved crew sliding up, cutting a swath in the silver sand. As we got out, Sandra discovered her knee was painful, and my feet and ankles were aching from being so cramped and immobile for hours. Sandra named the place 'Robinson Crusoe Island'. A brief reccie around the beach head (half expecting to encounter 'Man Friday'), crunching our wet feet through the piles of stranded, bleached driftwood, found us a tranquil spot behind some bushes. We made our first camp on a

ten foot wide strip of glistening white sand, bordered on one side
by the bushes; the other side dropped steeply down into a narrow
creek. On our journey we passed many such creeks of varying
widths. Their purpose appeared to be irrigation of the reclaimed
land bordering the Gironde. The hundreds of square miles of flat
farmland were protected from the river by a massive dyke that
followed the course of the river. The top of the dyke had a rough
track along which we very occasionally saw someone on a scooter
or bumping along in a car. Intriguingly, jutting out at intervals
along the dyke, there were lots of huts on sticks which we later
discovered are called 'carrelet' and used for fishing with a large
round net on a hoop. Our small two-man tent was pitched next to
some large logs that had been deliberately set in a rectangle. In the
centre were the black charcoal remains of a camp fire. In a matter
of minutes we had hung our wet things on the bushes and brewed
up. Now warm and sunny, Sandra donned her bikini and, using the
logs as rustic furniture, we sat together eating some of our supplies
..... bananas, nuts, and chocolate raisins. As we chomped
ravenously on these delicacies, a couple of old style wooden
sailing boats, creaking with the sound of oars in rollicks,
materialised from the creek. They were being rowed by a
compliment of young girls who, once they reached the main
stream, set their sails and disappeared down stream with the
ebbing tide. The water was well on its way out, leaving exposed
mud banks and small channels of water. It caused us to ponder
over the question, 'How were they going to get back?' Walking
boots on, we left the canoe next to the tent, our kit stowed and
covered by the canvas decking, and set off to see where the inlet
would lead us. A little intimate country bar serving French wine
and cheese was the image drifting through our minds as we walked
the two miles or so through deserted fields before arriving at a
small, inland, quayside village. The navigable creek ended there
at a sluice gate. The three or four grey stone houses lining the
minute mooring area appeared to be empty. The wooden shutters
were tight shut, and the occupants were obviously battened down
for the night. Some distant dogs barked way off across the fields
somewhere, and dreams of our first taste of French wine and
cheese instantly dissolved. A brief nose around the ghost town,

and we made our way back to our 'campsite' where we enjoyed a cosy cooked meal of an instant sachet of risotto with an instant tin of sardines, followed by a couple of sweets. To bed! ..... a good night's deep sleep, cocooned in our new mini sleeping bags, lying, instead of sitting, on our new, wonderfully comfortable mattresses.

DAY TWO: Wednesday 14th July

Fresh, inspired and revived, we were up at first light, 6.30am, to admire the huge, fiery red ball of a rising sun, like a huge tomato on the horizon. Sandra said that she had heard the waves during the night and that the sky looked magical when she got up to use the 'en suite bush'. I had to admit that I saw no stars and heard no waves ..... I was dead to the world. To our surprise, the tide was still going out! Sandra concluded therefore (Sandra was the tide chart expert - I found it as unfathomable as trying to read a bus timetable) that it must have come in again during the night, and then turned before we awoke. From this state of affairs, Sandra deduced that we now had to wait until 1.30pm before it came back in sufficiently for us to re-launch. I felt a wave of peace ripple over me ..... we were unrushed and we could spend a little more time in this beautiful spot. Strolling leisurely around the beach, I noticed that the sand had a curious consistency and sparkling appearance. Kneeling, I took a handful to examine, and on closer scrutiny, I discovered that it was in fact made up of crushed oyster shells, obviously created over many, many years by the active local fishing industry. We pondered over why they had been crushed to grains, and marvelled at the tiny pieces of mother of pearl that attractively and magically twinkled as they caught the sun. Sandra recollected our visit to a windy bay on the west coast of Australia, just south of Monkey Mia, called Shell Beach which stretches for 110 kilometres, and is made up of five metre deep tiny white cockleshells! This white shingle is quarried and used for gardens and public parks as an attractive dressing and to retain moisture. Breakfast took place ..... Jordan's straight from the packet, swilled down with big mugs of hot tea. We had plenty of water and compact food substances stowed on board, and it was a most satisfying and reassuring feeling to be detached from civilisation, whilst enjoying the challenge of self-reliance. Mind you, we had only been travelling a day and were still carrying the body fat of our glutinous western live styles. I felt healthier for adding dried skimmed milk to my tea, and made a resolution, there and then, that, I would no longer take my usual milk with breakfast.

COCKLESHELLS COMPO

Compared to ours, the Heroes' rations were pretty dire to say the least. Their food supply was far from satisfactory. It was of the compact rations type. Each man had three wax cardboard cartons for the day, each consisting of a small tin of mixed tea leaves, powered milk, and sugar which, by throwing into boiling water, produced a ready-made mug of tea. In addition, each man had a small tin of cheese, and another of a meat mixture similar to Spam, also biscuits, sweets, cigarettes, chewing gum, and lifeboat fuse matches. The food was unpalatable and lacked bulk; in fact none of them ever ate the whole day's ration and saved the leftovers for their escape. One interesting item was a block of compressed oatmeal which could be made into porridge, if it was possible to cook; otherwise it was chewed as a hard cake.

SIGHT SEEING

Photograph: Dyke, spikes and cat

We allocated our 'waiting for the tide to turn' hours by walking one mile back along the dyke ridge gravel cart track to the Phare de Richard disused lighthouse. We were surprised to come in contact with civilisation, finding the building was now a museum and open to the public. The lighthouse was run by jovial voluntary staff who gave an interesting commentary, obviously in French, but with Sandra's more than adequate command, and my limited, i.e. 'petit pois, fromage, je voudrais une glace' type scratchy knowledge, we were able to easily decipher the salient points and get the gist …..'La Gironde is the largest estuary in Europe and spans 13 kilometers at its widest point. The channel is constantly dredged as it gets so silted up with mud' ….. hence our encounters with the menacing dredger! Climbing to the top of the lighthouse afforded us a bird's eye view of the river, and the reclaimed land, covered in farm crops and vineyards established by English businessmen in the early 1900's for the wine industry. The interior of the rotund brick walls inside the building were regaled with dozens of old photographs, portraying a vivid visual history of the area. It enlightened us to the fact that, when the Cockleshell Heroes landed in this area, they would have witnessed a busy and thriving oyster industry. The shoreline of sticking up posts was left over from that era.

COCKLESHELLS FIRST HIDE

Now 'Catfish' and 'Crayfish' landed at Pointe aux Oiseaux at daybreak on Wednesday 8th December 1942. During the dangerous, daylight hours, Major Hasler and his men lay on the shore, dispersed amongst their canoes and camouflage nets. Desperately, they attempted to be as inconspicuous as was possible on this bleak, flat landscape. However, it seemed they were being observed by the fishermen and women (from the Ardouin and Chaussat families of St. Vivien). The routine in those days was that the fishermen of St. Vivien would sail their fishing boats down the creek into La Gironde and come ashore in their dinghies to find their wives and families, having arrived on oxcarts, preparing breakfast over log fires for their fishermen before they set forth into the Bay of Biscay. Obviously it was not long before they noticed the Commandos. This was their first contact with the French. Hasler, heart pounding in his chest, thinking on his stomach, decided to break cover and approach them. In his fluent, but limited French, he explained to them that they were English, on a secret mission, and asked for their help and secrecy. (Hasler was aware of a certain apprehension from the French whenever he had the occasion to dialogue with them. Much later, whilst in the company of the French Resistance, they pointed out that his public school brogue gave him a German accent every time he spoke French, thus explaining their anxiety). After a brief, animated conflab between the fishermen and their women, a representative (M. Yves Ardouin) promised their discretion, and kindly advised Hasler to move his task force further along the river bank, out of sight of German sentries engaged in the construction of a military installation nearby. These kind peasant people gave them a little food and protected them by their silence. After the war, Hasler and Sparks returned to St Vivien to visit the families who, in pain of certain death if caught by the Germans, had helped them.

REVEALING

Rambling our way back to the site of our bivouac, we could see that the tide had turned and the water was now beginning to ripple back. It was unsettling for us to observe, still protruding from the muddy quagmire, a proliferation of sharp, rotten and lethal looking wooden stakes, tree trunks, tangled rusty wire, and goodness only knows what else, littering the river bed. For a few minutes we sat on the low, dry stone wall that stretched the complete length of the dyke. Trance-like, we silently absorbed the atmosphere of the fields laid out behind us, and the magnificent river to our front with all this debris and dangerous obstacles that were normally submerged at high tide. With this perilous picture now well and truly imbedded in our subconscious minds, we discussed the plight of the members of Operation Frankton.

A FATAL ACCIDENT

Mackinnon and Conway, who became separated from Hasler in the early stages of the Operation, with much determination, and unknown to Hasler until after the war, had continued on their own and had even rested just a short distance away from Hasler and Laver on the Ile de Cazeau. Unfortunately, whilst Mackinnon and Conway were attempting the last leg of the journey, their flimsy canvas canoe was snagged and severely torn by some ghastly submerged obstructions (probably like those we had observed). This episode eventually proved fatal for them. The canoe was wrecked and quickly began to sink. Conway only just managed to extricate himself as it went under, and they both swam back to the island and eventually, after an almost successful escape bid, were captured and left to the mercy of the Nazis. Almost to Bilbao and a boat home to safety, Lt Mackinnon developed a nasty, festering boil on his knee. The Resistance refused to move them until it was treated. Once in hospital, they were betrayed, sent to Paris and handed over to the Gestapo who put them through a brutal three month inquisition until the end of March, whereupon failing to extort any information, they were mercilessly taken out and shot.

LEAVING 'CRUSOE ISLAND'

With those details in mind, we both breathed an individual sigh of relief, mine that there were no Nazis looking for us, and Sandra's that our vessel was constructed of a strong, acrylic material. However, we were not so complacent or blind to the fact, having noticed the deep scratches already sustained to the bottom of the Sardine (caused by dragging it across sharp stones and shells), that we were not totally immune to this problem. In anticipation of such a situation, I had packed my own (more economical than those on sale in the boating shops) canoe repair kit. This was a good old reliable Woolworths shoe sole repair kit. The contents consisted of two large man's sized rubber soles, one small rectangular metal abrasive device for preparing the surface, and one tube of excellent adhesive that I find suitable for almost anything. There was just time for another brew up and a brief sunbathe on our 'Robinson Crusoe Island'. We then ferried all our gear to the foreshore, dragged the canoe down and frantically stowed it. The water was now visibly moving up the beach, lapping at all our dry stuff and rising rapidly up our legs. Having misjudged the waves slightly on the launch shove, we received a bit of a showering as a wave broke over us before I had quite fixed the canvas decking ..... not too perturbed 'though, as it was warm water. Glancing back, the pearly sand was glistening in the sun.

SECOND LEG

We felt stronger and exhilarated by our rest up, yet a little sad to be leaving such a beautiful spot. Being so warm and sunny, we wore tee shirts and life ..... sorry, 'buoyancy aids' and shorts only. At first, we had a repeat of our landmark navigational and recognition difficulties, but as the shipping channel veered south, we found ourselves in it and came across our first sighting of the red and green channel marker buoys. However, the buoys were a long way apart, and as we paddled, they remained frustratingly and endlessly in the distance. With perfectly synchronised paddle strokes, and the mesmerising sound of the water against our bows, we calmly glided along, basking in the warm sunshine. Just like the day before, we were again the only craft on the river, and the distant shoreline appeared to be deserted. Such a huge expanse of water with just us on it! Sandra liked being in front, enjoying the uninterrupted view, whilst having the security that I was behind paddling whenever she wanted a break. In contrast, my rear view position was constantly obscured by the back of her head and combat cap! I preferred to paddle for longer periods.

Major Hasler, as front man, spoke after the mission of the strange, illogical and irrationally malevolent feelings and thoughts that he occasionally developed towards his rear man, Sparks. During their endless hours of silent paddling in the dark, Hasler would imagine that Sparks wasn't paddling, or that he was turning round to look for the other canoes, and these, together with other unjust thoughts and psychological mind tricks, sometimes even drove him to actually consider twisting round to deal Sparks a sharp blow with his paddle. Fortunately, he managed to contain himself.

Way in the distance on the horizon, veiled in a heat haze, we could see a huge 'Fairy Castle'. Together, we let our imaginations wander preposterously, musing over improbable scenarios. Perhaps Rapunzel would appear at a turret window, let down her hair, and be rescued by a bold, armour-clad knight on a white charger. Or, we would be invited in by a baron to enjoy a medieval banquet, the comedy of a court jester, and the dulcet tunes of minstrels. Sadly and unromantically, we later realised that it was the nuclear power station!

TEMPTATION

A couple of hours paddling and we both simultaneously noticed what appeared to be a large building on the shore to our right, or starboard, to those precious about such nautical details. It was probably a quarter of a mile or so to the shore from where we were, so visual recognition with the bare eye was not totally reliable. Binoculars would have been useful at that moment, but just before we left home, the left lens fell out of ours and they became 'mono-oculars'. In any case, they were the old large field glasses type and would have been too cumbersome. A discussion ensued as to whether or not it was a restaurant with a blue awning and white chairs standing on a green lawn rolling down to the waters edge, or was it a mirage? Hunger and thirst took command of our wiser instincts. A quick assessment of the facts, i.e. the tide time left in our favour and the distance we had yet to cover that day, led us to a unanimous decision. We engaged our sharpest starboard turn, and made a frantic bid for the shore before we could be swept past it. Drawing close, we could see a small inlet surrounded by a sleepy little harbour village. We had been following the church spires, water towers, and other prominent landmarks on the chart, so gauged we were in St Christoly-Medoc. On our approach to the long, raked, grey stone harbour wall (mole), we passed a man fishing and a small boy wearing bright orange armbands, swimming back and forth. Once we were alongside the sloping harbour wall, we grabbed hold of one of the tangled web of mooring ropes. I released the canvas decking, rummaged inside the Sardine, and extracted, from just by my left ankle, our new blue nylon rope, and although I say so myself, I was quite pleased with my first (haven't done it for years), most professional tying up job of the trip. I devised a slip knot so that the rope could remain secured to the bows, but still be released from the shore whilst sitting in the Sardine. This erased the farcical procedure of untying, pushing off and simultaneously jumping in. We had a glance around the town centre which boasted a lovely ornate church, butchers, boulangerie, hairdressers, petrol station, and, bliss ..... three people. We wandered back to the only restaurant, and after a little deliberation, we chose from the menu board outside. Entering the restaurant, salivating expectantly for the cheese and wine awaiting us, we were greeted by the large, apron wearing, moustached landlord, snorting "Ferme! Ferme!" ..... well, after all, it was past 4pm! So much for 'entente cordiale'. Slightly deflated, we returned to the quay where a mature madame was selling various drinks from the front of her house, so we sat on her white cast iron garden furniture, under the shade of a Coca-Cola parasol. Excitedly, we pointed to names of drinks, none of which were familiar to us, from a list on a display board. She shortly appeared with a strong chestnut coloured liqueur of varnish consistency, and a cool beer. Absorbing the view and tasting each other's drinks was most relaxing, but we had to go hungry. A man walked past tantalisingly with a loaf of crusty bread pinned under his arm, and that image, along with the slightly scruffy buildings, shuttered windows, and a smoky old Renault car rattling by over the cobbled street, meant we just had to be in rural, laid back France. 'Ooh la, la. Formidable!'

LA GIRONDE SPOKE

Photograph: Saved by the creek

Slipping out of the smooth inlet, we were surprised to be confronted by gigantic waves and a fierce head-on wind. During our short rest period, the wind had got up, and the river had changed into an angry, tossing torrent. We had intended crossing to the other bank to Portes de Callonge, the Heroes' second stop. Pitching full ahead into the two foot high choppy waves sent the water cascading over the Sardine, soaking down through our waist bands to our shorts. It also permeated through the Velcro seams of the canvas decking on to our legs. We soon became swamped, sitting in pools of water, and it became terrifyingly obvious that it was too dangerous to continue on this tack. We kept our heads down and pushed forward, but always slightly to the left (port, for the nautically sensitive) into the tide until we reached the centre channel. Looking ahead at the vast distance we still had to cover to reach the other side, and the increasingly frenzied state of the water, we decided rather rapidly not to attempt the crossing but to engage our contingency plan. The task was now to look for a suitable place to stop on the west bank. Watching for the slightest lull in the waves, we took our lives literally in our hands and engaged our well rehearsed sharp right turn (to prevent a broadside wave capsizing us). We were now being washed along with the stream. It was very exciting and exhilarating 'surfing' on some of the waves which we could hear breaking behind us. It would have been great to get an action photograph, so trying to hold my paddle under my arm-pit and steer at the same time, I attempted to locate the camera. It was just below the canvas decking against my hip, but even so, things were so frantic that there was absolutely no chance of me grabbing hold of it without losing the paddle and our stability. There was no let up, the waves were relentless, and in the turmoil we had forgotten about our hunger, but we were making good speed. At the same time, we had to keep our wits about us and not lose concentration. It took all the strength that we could muster to remain upright and on course. All the while the river was pushing us towards the bank where there was even more turbulence due to the merciless pounding of the waves against the tall, solid wall of green reeds. We realised the tide had turned, so wind against tide made matters even worse. This was our first experience of the changing tide in La Gironde. Until now, we had worked out a pattern of paddling whereby every now and then one of us would take a short break whilst the other continued, and after an hour (like the Heroes) we would have a short break, but not on this occasion, even 'though we began to tire. Nearly exhausted, hands and arms aching, and soaked, but not actually cold, I glanced down to check our position on the chart. During our ridged focus on the tumultuous job in hand, I hadn't noticed that the chart case, although still hanging safely from my neck on its nylon cord, had been dragging in the water. Even 'though the Velcro seal was tight, capillary attraction had allowed a film of water to seep inside and across the surface of the chart. Fortunately, it was coated with a waterproof surface. Unfortunately, it didn't display all the little inlets and creeks, but where there was one of a reasonable size, then it was shown. Pitching our voices above the wave and wind din, we debated our next overnight stop. With the tide turning against us, we knew that we couldn't keep going for much longer. There was a definite creek clearly defined on the chart, but because we only knew roughly where we were, we weren't quite sure how far it was from our present location. In any case, with the density of the thick, towering reeds massed along the bank, there was just nowhere for us to even hove-to for a breather. Our spirits began to slowly ebb, and just a little fear set in. Clouds obscured the sun, making it slightly darker, adding a more sinister view to our predicament. We could feel the ferocity of the tide becoming quickly stronger beneath us, and worries were creeping into our minds, making us impatient, sapping our strength, eroding logical thought and judgement. Having battled on for so long, the thought of being swept all the way back would be a total disaster. On top of that fear was the fact that there was just nowhere amongst the barrier of reeds for us to pull in and escape the continuous pounding, so we just had to keep going. Hope was raised when we spotted a small inlet amongst the reeds, dropping again when we realised it wasn't the charted one, and in any case, there was no landing place. Near breaking point, our prayers were answered. We almost missed the marked creek because of the density of the reeds, but the Heroes must have proffered guidance and helped us manoeuvre the Sardine into a good position. Paddling like demons, using our new found energy summoned by the promise of an escape route, coupled with an instant morale boost, we broke free of the vicious river and slipped gently into another dimension! It was like a mill pond in shape and atmosphere. As if the cruel river had to have the last word, a large wave rolled in behind us, washing across the deck.

RELIEF AT LAST ..... OUR SECOND CAMP

At approximately 6.45pm, after five and a quarter hours paddling (less a forty five minute break), we now found ourselves in a tranquil haven, relaxing into our seats. Like Anthony and Cleopatra in their majestic barge on the Nile, we drifted serenely along the reed-lined banks of the tributary, led by a royal entourage of five small ducks. Roughly a quarter of a mile further on, we approached some large, dominating, steel, double lock gates. They had been built into a half moon shaped red brick retaining wall, topped off with flat white cement coping stones. Above the gates ran a road bridge carrying a small section of a quiet country road. A flurry of paddles sent us urgently forward, ramming our bows into a mud bank. This action served to anchor and hold us fast temporarily, whilst we both crawled forward over the Sardine and up on to the steep grassy bank, running off in different directions to do a sweeping reccie. Minutes later, we returned to find the Sardine almost vertical, stern submerged by the weight of the cargo almost to the open cockpit, and its bows high and dry on a small island of mud. Incredibly, in that short period, the water had drained away leaving steep sloping mud banks. Unfurling the long bow rope, and pulling it over our shoulders, together we heaved, dragging the laden Sardine squeaking from the deep slimy brown mud, up and over the six foot parapet cliff-like river bank, and into the waist high rough grass of the adjoining wasteland.

GLORIOUS MUD

For the men of Operation Frankton, the experience of these mud banks was, in contrast to ours, much, much worse. Launching was a wet, cold and dirty business. Typically, the muddy beach stretched up fifty feet or so to a steep mud cliff. Hasler and Sparks slid, literally, from the top of the cliff, landing thigh deep in the icy, oozing mud. Laver and Mills would then lower the two canoes down to them, and slide down to join the others. They would all push their canoes over the soft squelchy beach to the waters edge. Caked in the filthy muck, and wet through up to the waist, they would crawl back into their respective crafts, and make off, dissolving into the dark murky waters.

CAMOUFLAGE AND CONCEALMENT

Photograph: Number 2 camp, Where's the Sardine?

With me pulling and Sandra pushing, the Sardine slid through the tall rough grass until it was in a good inconspicuous spot, away from the road, and about fifteen metres from the edge of the river bank. Offering a complete contrast to what we had left behind in the river, apart from the birds chattering away on a wire, there was complete silence, and we were bathed in the last of the warm sun. A village could be seen on a slight hill some two or so miles away. The Sardine was speedily unpacked, tent erected in record time, and all our wet clothes strewn discretely (so as not to be seen from the road) on the ample vegetation to dry. Sandra discovered the dye from the gaily coloured beach towel she'd been sitting on had run into her clothes, right down to her undies! Cautious not to lose anything, especially the Sardine, we covered everything completely with big bunches of the abundant long grass. With our camp camouflaged and concealed, we set off for the town and fresh food, or at least something alcoholic. It was a lovely balmy evening stroll along a classic country lane winding through a wood of bushy green trees. Occasionally, as we progressed, there were narrow breaks in the wood for a path or grassy track. Through these gaps we caught a glimpse of the river beyond, reminding us of its perpetual presence. A friendly chestnut horse nodded to us over a gate, and we fraternised with him for a while, feeding him grass from our open palmed hands. To him, the grass was much tastier and greener than on his side. Passing the beautifully kept uniform rows of vines that stretched out across the peaceful land, together we ambled happily along. Just below the village, before we climbed the last five hundred metres up the old single carriage ironed road, we passed a very large collection of top-of-the-range expensive travellers' caravans and motor vehicles. They were pitched on a large field below the town which afforded a marvellous view out over the river. A couple of the occupants approached us. They looked rather surly, possibly of eastern European origin, but we kept walking purposefully as they gabbled away in a language that we couldn't identify. We hoped they weren't going to follow and pester us, or the worst scenario, mug us. Our, "Sorry, no comprehend," reply in English was met with an open-mouthed silent stare, as they stood glued to the road watching us walk away. There was a group of gendarmes gathered, talking to some of the occupants of one of the caravans, and that seemed to be our salvation. Upon reaching the quaint little village, we discovered we were in St. Estephe, but to our dismay, everything was shuttered and silent ..... it was, after all, nearly dark in rural France ..... so after a short walk around the church dominated centre, we ran the travellers' gauntlet once more, and returned to base. Camouflaging the tent and the Sardine might have appeared to be a rather dramatic measure. However, in view of the fact that only a mile or so away we had encountered hordes of itinerate travellers, it was retrospectively a wise move. It also reinforced our connection with the reality of Operation Frankton when Hasler and his men had to lay low during the day under their camouflage nets. In contrast to Hasler's daytime broken sleep, we were now preparing for bed in the dark. Unpolluted by any artificial lighting, the sky was crystal clear and encrusted with shimmering stars. A long-awaited supper of instant mash, with sardines stirred in, was cooked and eaten from our mess tins, whilst we both stood amongst the waist high foliage. Being so dark that I couldn't see the food, I wondered how many insects I had eaten. Before we had finished this tasty morsel, a gigantic firework display erupted on the opposite shore. It was obviously taking place in Portes de Callonge, right near the Cockleshells second stopping place and where we had so desperately tried to reach. It was an omen, and obviously no coincidence, but a direct sign to say that the Heroes were cheering us on, and that their spirits were following us. Fireworks continued throughout the night, and we later discovered that it was Bastille Day, but that was somebody else's revolution many years ago, and we prefer to believe our own theory!

DAY THREE: Thursday 15th July

Bleary eyed, aching and stiff limbed, we crawled from our claustrophobic accommodation to be welcomed by a wet early morning dew that lay heavy and sparkling on the thick jungle of grass engulfing our tent and the Sardine. Sandra had got out in the night for a pee and was attacked by our thatched roof, making her look like a scare crow! We also discovered that scrambling through the sharp blades of grass and tangled thorns of the undergrowth had left red weals and scratches all over our legs. Clouds of white vapour rose gently as the rising sun warmed the hedgerows and vines. Stretching our bodies in the slight morning chill, we could feel the promise of a fine day. After a meagre breakfast, we broke camp fast and stowed all our gear into the Sardine. We covered it with the damp vegetation, and ran over to check that it could not be seen from the road. Of course, we had to wait for the tide again which advanced an hour every day. The walk back to St Estephe appeared quicker, as it does when one knows the way. To our astonishment, the travellers had vanished in the night, leaving neat piles of black bin sacks at irregular intervals around the deserted and relatively clean field. St Estephe had arisen, not quite bustling, but the few locals were now awake and going about their daily business. This was the first opportunity for us to go shopping so we purchased a padlock, some fresh food and, of course, a bottle of the local vintage. Sprawled at a table outside a quaint French café, at last indulging in the decadent pleasures of cheese and wine, and basking in hot sunshine, we observed the local culture and traditions. All it amounted to, from our perspective, was wandering around clutching sticks of bread, and chatting with friends at the corner of rustic buildings. I found that very easy to live with, and definitely a lifestyle I could adapt to. On the church door was a sign saying, 'Open to all faiths on Sunday', in three different languages. As it was only Thursday, we gingerly opened the vast, intricately carved, creaky wooden door to be beckoned in by the verger. We gazed at the colourful, but gory wall paintings with images portraying the many torturous punishments of hell, and the lavishly embossed gold leaf refinery, before returning with our loaves, but no fishes, to the humble Sardine.

THE THIRD LEG

Fully laden ..... now with the addition of a bottle of French wine stowed underneath the sleeping bag on Sandra's right side, and an extra bottle of drinking water beneath the left-hand sleeping bag ..... we pushed the Sardine across the bank, gently tipped it over the steep, perpendicular ridge and down into the muddy quagmire. At 2.45pm, rocking ourselves forward in our seats, we slid about thirty five feet down the mud ..... like a Disney log flume ride in slow motion! Pushing our oars into the deep thick mud (finding it difficult to pull them out again!), we slithered, like a furtive ridged crocodile, back into the water, and floated out of the inlet, once more into La Gironde. The river had narrowed by now, so we braved it and took advantage of the fast flowing centre channel. We approached what appeared to be an old armchair tumbling along with the current. Clipping our paddles, it skimmed by, a little too close for comfort, and turned out to be a solid, rotten tree trunk. This was nothing unusual ..... we had already seen, and would still have to avoid, tons more driftwood and miscellaneous items of discarded rubbish. Very dangerous.

COMPARISON

Again, we associated this particular scenario with the Cockleshell Heroes. Whilst they were stealthily planting their limpet mines on one of the enemy ships in Bordeaux, a German sentry on board looked over the side of the ship, straight down to where they were. Hasler and Sparks, hearing the studs of his jack boots on the iron deck directly above them, immediately froze. The sentry shone his torch right on to them for a terrifying moment. Then, possibly thinking that he was looking at flotsam and jetsam, he switched off his torch and moved away, clanking back across the deck. When I read about that detail in the account of the Operation, it didn't seem feasible. However, having seen so much wood and trash floating up and down the river, I can now quite understand the sentry's mistake.

BUOYANT

Photograph: Aproaching buoy 38

Even 'though we were paddling towards mid-river, by the time we reached it, we had been washed downstream a whole mile which again reminded us of the strength of the tide. Navigation became easier as each of the green and red marker buoys had a number painted on it, and all these numbers were obviously printed on the chart. Therefore I deduced that, by calibrating the number displayed on the buoy with that shown on the chart, we should know our exact position. From there on we identified all the buoys, confirming them with our chart and current location. Moving closer to an anchored buoy to take its photograph was an unnerving experience as it appeared to be hurtling towards us at a great rate of knots, producing a tremendous wash behind it. It resembled some kind of space station, with a large bulbous base, steel braced tower, and lamp perched on top. We were afraid it might hit us, but of course it was the Sardine with us on board that was being propelled by the fierce tide towards the buoy. It brought home to us just how strong the current actually was, and how we needed to watch our steering! The photographic record of buoy number 38 confirmed our sighting of the Cockleshell Heroes second hide point, just north of Portes de Callonge. Alone as usual, it was so peaceful just drifting along. How different from the previous afternoon's experience! The absence of breeze, together with hot sunshine beating down and reflecting on the water, made our plastic life-jackets stick to us, but we resisted the temptation of disguarding them. We also discovered later that despite using sun screen, Sandra had a red nose and swollen lips, and I had sunburnt arms.

THE DESERT ISLAND

We passed the town of Pauillac on our right with its predictable dominant church, lovingly renovated wine chateau, and surrounding vineyards. The chateau, like many others, was in the style of a typical rectangular stately pile, with flying cylindrical turrets attached to all four corners. Each turret wore a pointed, cone shaped, grey slate leaded roof. They reminded me of the Tin Man's hat in 'The Wizard of Oz'. The water seemed muddier than usual and was swirling with eddies. We sailed between some delightful islands that were covered with lots of vegetation, and alongside Vasard de Beychevelle where the Heroes, who nicknamed it 'Desert Island', had stopped for six hours.

Being restricted to moving under the cover of darkness, Major Hasler had been forced to halt his warriors on the island after travelling for only three hours on the flood tide. That meant that they had to sit out a six hour tide turn around. Continuing their journey along narrow channels between islands, Hasler and his men moved with the greatest caution, uncomfortable that the noise of their dipping paddles would be heard. From the shore, even 'though it was dark, they could now see and hear the sights and sounds of people, traffic, and normal every day life emanating from the villages as they passed. Within this dangerously close proximity, they had been praying for rain or wind to dissipate the sound of their paddles, but it hadn't come. Unnervingly, they were alarmed by the sudden sound of a motor boat engine starting up. Scuttling away towards the island bank, both canoes went crashing into the cover of the tall reeds. There they remained, the crews' heads hard down on to the decks, motionless, hearts throbbing, until the phantom boat had passed them by. The shadowy launch had aroused their suspicions and perhaps provoked a little paranoia. It had no lights, and so they wondered if it was searching for them. Whatever the answer, they didn't wait to find out, and under the cover of its engine noise still reverberating across the water, they slipped out from the curtain of reeds and continued swiftly on their way.

IN SIGHT OF BLAYE

The spectre of the nuclear power station (unimaginable at the time of Operation Frankton) still dominated the left (east) bank and did so for ages. Every now and then, I would sit back with my face towards the sun, and dip my sunburnt arms in the cool river water which was most refreshing. Lying directly behind, east, and slightly longer than 'Desert Island', we now saw 'Ile Nouvelle', and beyond that, nestling below its magnificent Citadelle, was the town of Blaye.

It was to Blaye that the four surviving Heroes, namely Hasler, Sparks, Laver and Mills, returned after the attack, scuttled their canoes and made their brave escape. For obvious reasons, they split into two groups. Major Hasler and Sparks were the most fortunate party. After completing a gruelling wet hundred mile walk in freezing conditions, and after several months, with help from the Resistance, they eventually made good their escape, via the Pyrenees, down through Spain to Gibraltar, and finally to dear old Blighty. For Laver and Mills, things didn't go so well. Unlike Hasler and Sparks, they were unable to locate, or cadge, any civilian clothes. Although they had made good headway through very rough terrain for two days, covering some twenty miles, they were picked up by the French police (on the 14th December 1942) in Montlieu La Garde, a suburb of Montlieu twelve miles south-east of the hamlet of Villexavier through which Hasler and Sparks had passed on the very same day. They were handed over to the German security police and went on to suffer the terrible and predictable fate meeted out by the Nazis. The callous use of subterfuge of sparing their lives during interrogation was carried out in accordance with the direct orders of Adolf Hitler who demanded that they be shot after being questioned, 'with no methods barred'. After three months in the unscrupulous hands of the Germans (gallantly disclosing nothing), they were finally executed on the 23rd March 1942 in Paris.

OUR THIRD BIVVY

Photograph: Mooring in Blaye

Blaye was to be our first stop on the opposite (east) bank. In trying to secure a good photograph of the Citadelle, we overshot the landing point and were swept away by the tide, ending up alongside a cargo ship that was loading grain. Feverish paddling ensued as we tried frantically, and in vain, to go against the current. A group of stevedores working on the ship found our predicament a great laugh. From their position, we must have looked most comical as we paddled and paddled, like two demented hamsters in a spinning treadmill, only to remain stationary. Frustrated and humiliated in front of our guffawing audience, a heated exchange of ideas passed between the crew of the Sardine. Paddles now motionless, we drifted defeated downstream with the current, sculling round behind the stern of the ship. Discretely, and out of sight of our tormentors, we hugged the shoreline, free of the tide, and entered the low (perhaps four feet between the surface of the water and ceiling), narrow, eerie space beneath the pontoon. Out of the sun, it felt cool in the shadows of the overwhelming structure. The massive girth of the closely knit concrete supports left us with barely a few inches to spare on either side, so we hastily withdrew our paddles, and grappling with our bare hands, we gingerly edged our way forward through the confines of the cramped, claustrophobic space. Occasionally the movement of the men working above would cause grain to filter through fine gaps in the decking and on to our heads. Emerging on the other side, we were met by a mother duck, accompanied by a solitary chick frantically paddling and weaving erratically like a fluffy wind-up toy. Next, we were confronted by the tremendous wash that was emanating from the river crossing ferry as it manoeuvred on to its jetty, now right ahead of our bows. We bounced up and down in the frothy, foaming wash, precariously close to the stone sea defence, along with some basking ducks who soon took to the water when the waves arrived. Eventually the water settled down and under the jetty we paddled, edging our way along, like a commando raid (in character for the theme of our trip), past a huge trapped log, and in-between the 'ghost train'-like struts of the jetty, much to the amusement of the ferrymen. It seemed as 'though we had become great entertainment for the local mariners. Thankfully we found ourselves turning into a quay whereupon we pulled the Sardine on to the stone slipway which formed part of the dock. At the same time, a small private fishing vessel arrived and tied up to a floating mooring buoy. The owners came ashore in a minute fibreglass dinghy and happily spilled out on to the quay. After silently mouthing her routine, Sandra bravely approached the middle-aged owner, and in unfaltering fluent French (to me anyway), she managed to gain his pleasing permission to raft the Sardine alongside his boat. As we had intended to leave some of our stuff inside the hull, this arrangement made it less accessible and gave us a little more security. Having purchased an eighteen foot long, small gauge security chain in England, I had overlooked the requirement of a padlock. Therefore, it was a good job that I had managed to purchase one in St Estephe. The owner of the boat was most friendly and obliging. Still bearing our historic, English traditional dislike of the French, it was with pleasurable surprise that all our canoeing encounters with this independent race turned out to be, without exception, beyond the call of duty, amicable, and helpful. It took some gymnastic, acrobatic manoeuvres on my part to moor the Sardine, but once it was safely rafted, locked, and chained alongside the French boat and to the mooring chains lying on the quay, we bade farewell to our newly acquired French acquaintance and made for 'Betty's Bar'. This haven of gastronomic delights was situated tantalisingly on the opposite side of an adjoining road, a short walk across a rusty disused railway line. At the time of the Cockleshell Heroes, this overgrown railway line would have been alive with goods steam trains servicing the many ships that, because of modern replacement forms of transport, are no more than ghosts of a long since past and distant way of life. It was also a time of different values, morals, and countries and cultures that were worth dying for. 'Betty's Bar' was to fulfil a longing that had motivated me whilst I was paddling in the hot sun. My first cold, dripping wet with condensation, glass of local on tap Blaye beer went down my parched throat in one quick, thirst quenching gulp. It reminded me of the last scene in the Second World War film, 'Ice Cold in Alex', when the actor, Sir John Mills, rewarded himself by gulping down a freezing glass of beer, having survived some near death, arduous, hot and sandy escapades with the Germans in the North African desert. With my drained glass, I was back to the bar for a refill, this time, to sit, sip and savour. We both felt blessed and so happy to be in such a picturesque place and safe haven.

COCKLESHELLS ESCAPE

Hasler and Sparks had no warm welcome in Blaye on that chilling December night. Having planted their limpet mines successfully on the enemy ships in the harbour of Bordeaux, they paddled hard, non-stop for nine hours, covering twenty six miles. Just short of the escape area, around about St Genes-de-Blaye, they parted with Laver and Mills, paddled against the young flood tide, and made for the shore. Wallowing up to the waist in the cold wet slime, they drew their knives and scuttled their trusty canoe by cutting open the buoyancy bags and slitting the canvas sides. With heavy hearts, Hasler and Sparks watched their old friend sink gracefully out of sight to a watery, but honourable, grave. Hot soup, rather than cold beer, would have been their preference. All they possessed was their escape equipment. This consisted of half a gallon of water and what was left of their rations, probably enough for two days. They also had two little plastic 'escape boxes' per man, containing a map of France painted on a silk handkerchief, some book matches printed with the V-sign and the name of the English manufacturers, some malted milk tablets, and several luminous toy compasses about the size of a farthing. They were also supplied with a pair of felt soled boots to replace their gym shoes, and thin soled waders which were no good for a long march. Their orders of escape were first, to obtain civilian clothes, and then to make for the town of Ruffec, located about seventy miles north of Bordeaux. Ruffec lies seventy miles north-east of Blaye. French escape organisations had been warned to expect them, and would have been on the look out for them at the approaches to Ruffec. This route was chosen because the Germans and Vichy police were looking for them on a direct route from Bordeaux to Spain.

ENJOYING BLAYE

On shanks pony ('a pied'), laden down like beasts of burden with all our camping kit, tent, sleeping bags, cooking stove, mess tins, provisions, change of clothes, vanity bag, etc., we made enquiries at the tiny Blaye Tourist Office just fifty metres from our mooring. In fluent English, Information directed us to 'camping', unbelievably right inside the majestic 17thC Citadelle, dominantly overlooking the town, the quay and La Gironde. A hot trek up the undulating cobbled causeway found us passing over and between two tremendously high, awe-inspiring masonry walls that encompassed the central structure. Their fifty metre or so thick footings gradually tapered off as they grew higher, and were crowned with a bastion that extended around the whole perimeter. Both walls were separated by a deep grass lined pit, perhaps originally excavated for a moat. Passing through the mighty portcullis gates, encumbered and chaffed by all our gear, we entered the inner sanctum of the castle. This consisted of several acres of narrow streets set in a grid, and lined with private accommodation blocks and small quaint cottages, restaurants – excellent crepes – and wine shops where we later tasted and purchased. Exploring deeper, we located a small, intimate, welcoming site, marked off into individual three sided camping bays by neat hedges of box shaped laurel bushes. The site peacefully accommodated a respectable, cosmopolitan bunch of campers ..... Germans, Irish, Danish, French etc, etc. We pitched the tent in our chosen 'garden' and, top priority, opened a bottle of Claret. The ritual of hammering malleable metal tent pegs with our rubber mallet into the lush green grass was a knuckle crunching task, as hidden below the turf lurked a bed of rock hard, flint stone impregnated earth. We cooked a noodle dish, and sitting on the grass under a beautifully flowering tree, we dined in the sunset (9.45pm), enjoying the warm evening air. Sandra had stomach cramp which she thought was probably due to dehydration and so we both drank plenty of water. Fresh water was now literally on tap, so we took advantage of the situation and wallowed luxuriously in a long, soothing shower, this being our first proper wash since leaving Port Bloc. We also took the opportunity of laundering our meagre supply of muddy, sweat stained clothes. Doby and ablutions complete, towels donned in toga and sarong wrap style, we wandered back to our pitch, stopping occasionally to chat with some of the other international holiday nomads. Enthralled by the various accounts of their peregrinations around Europe, they were equally interested in our journey, in particular the danger aspect. Having charged up the mobile in the washroom, text messages were sent home to tell everyone we were ok, as several of our friends had thought we were mad (and probably dead by now!). Almost instantly, it bleeped back with words of encouragement. Two sealed, waterproof plastic packages were opened for the first time. Mine contained a fresh set of basic clothes ..... one set of underwear, one pair of shorts, and a shirt. Sandra's also had 'ladies things'!

Feeling refreshed and squeaky clean, we ambled through the little medina of cafés housed within the Citadelle, and on down the cobbles to the quay to check on the Sardine. The quay was now totally drained, exposing a stone wall dropping ten to twelve feet to its muddy bottom, revealing to us just how deep it actually was. When we arrived at high tide, the water was in full flood, concealing the top of the quay wall, and at twenty foot intervals along its length, the top few rungs and hand rails of some iron access ladders were exposed. Reflecting back to our arrival, we had been under the misguided impression that it wasn't very deep, perhaps, we surmised at the time, waist high at the most. In fact, if I had slipped from the iron ladder that I had been so precariously balancing upon during my acrobatic endeavour to raft up the Sardine, I would most certainly have been completely submerged under the water. The twenty or so mixed bunch of old boats and new boats and all kinds of privately owned craft, neatly tethered, were all lying at odd angles on the mud bank where they had settled. Unlocking the new shiny brass padlock, I released the Sardine chain a few inches, allowing the bow to slip down level with the others. Just a few inches out ..... not bad ..... a good guess, I deduced. Returning to base camp, we rested our aching limbs in bed, and sipped our obligatory nightcap of hot Horlicks.

With the tent flap open in the balmy night air, we gazed up at the twinkling stars and magnificent Milky Way. What an idyllic place. We also mused over the fact that whilst Hasler was in training, a scientist acquaintance who was a wizard with a chemistry set, offered him some night vision drops that he had rustled up in a test tube. In character, Hasler dutifully applied them before several night exercises. Result - predictable - sore red eyes, but not better night vision! We also wondered what thoughts had gone through the Heroes' minds as they lay in hiding during the day, looking up at the featureless, bleak winter sky. Not, 'what an idyllic place', I'll be bound!

DAY FOUR: Friday 16th July

We had a lay in until 8am and then took final advantage of the site facilities. The two adjoining toilet blocks, being typically French, each catered for both sexes. Although everyone was very polite, Sandra found it strange cleaning her teeth next to a man shaving. We indulged in a little sunbathing in our secluded camping area whilst noshing a healthy breakfast and updating our logs. Like two members of an exclusive fitness club lounging in a sauna, the perspiration trickled in shiny beads over our flesh. This had the effect of de-toxing any nasty body impurities, or so we liked to think. Whatever, there was no doubt that we were a lot fitter, lithe, and the excesses of modern day life had been burned off with our regular exercise, a balanced, modest but healthy diet, plus the warm sunny weather. Physically and mentally we were on top of the world. We broke camp and wandered around the ancient ramparts of the historic fort, absorbing the panoramic view of the river below, before making our way, like a couple of pack ponies, back into town. Approaching the waterless quay, we saw a delinquent youth thoughtlessly engaged in the game of sploshing great lumps of concrete down into the slime. On reaching our mooring, we were horrified to find both the Sardine and the French boat splattered with mud. Ironically, with all the potential dangers of collision with flotsam and jetsam, etc, in the river, this puerile act of mindless vandalism could so easily have scuppered and sabotaged our expedition. It obviously amused the yob, but it would have been fatal for our delicate craft had a bolder hit it, and fortunately he left before doing any serious damage. Worried that the owner of the boat might suspect it was us who had made the ghastly mess on his vessel, Sandra deftly scribbled a short note in French mitigating us, and we left it for him to read upon his return. The sun was blazing down from a clear blue sky, and the heat was tremendous as we scrambled up and down the hot steel ladder to reload the Sardine. Getting everything back into the same position was essential for balance and comfort. The technique was probably very comical to the voyeur, but for us, it could be irritatingly tiresome, and because of the canoe's restricted capacity, never seemed to get any easier. To get some of our camping things back into their allocated positions required taking some of the remaining items out each time, and then laboriously replacing them. Whilst the Sardine floated or sat in the mud, I would climb first into the rear open cockpit and stand, wobbling precariously, as Sandra reached out from the bank or quay with the gear which I would then pack. Taking my life in my hands, I would then step into the front cockpit and repeat the process. It was a back bending painful job and frustratingly time consuming, but it could not be rushed, even when we were working against the tide movements. Overcome with heat exhaustion, we left the loaded Sardine and crossed the disused railway line, where we bumped into two elderly English tourists who told us their car thermometer was registering an outside temperature of 37 degrees! Flaked out, we staggered into 'Betty's Bar' for a liquid revival under the refreshing breeze of a large oscillating fan.

OUR FOURTH LEG

With the tide moving on an hour each day, it meant we were unable to leave Blaye until 3.45pm, with barely enough water to float us out into the current. First we had to head across the river, then turn left and slip behind Ile Verte, the longest island on the Gironde. Approximately 100 metres from the tip of the island, we realised that we had seriously misjudged the speed of the tide and were going to be swept down the wrong side. The water state was so calm that we were under the misapprehension that the tide was weak. Despite our recent experiences, we still hadn't grasped the fact that under this calm exterior was a raging torrent. To correct our mistake, we paddled down stream against the current, hoping that we would make enough headway to be swept down the far side of the island. The idea proved hopeless; there was no way we could go against the current, so summoning up all our strength, we attempted to paddle straight ahead. This worked fine until we reached the sharp point at which the island separated the water along its respective banks. We seemed to be held in suspended animation on a weir-like force of water. After a few minutes of frantic paddling in the searing heat, we tired and were pushed back towards the nearside of the island where we rested under the shade of a tree on the shoreline to reassess the situation. Dragging the heavily laden Sardine across the narrow headland to the other side was realistically not worth the attempt. Our next strategy was to pull ourselves along the bank, gripping the rocks with our hands until we reached the very end of the island, where we swiftly engaged the paddles. The rocks were barely submerged in the shallow water, deflecting the paddles, preventing us from gaining any traction, and so we found ourselves slipping back to where we had started. Demoralised, Sandra said we would just have to travel down the 'wrong' side of the island, but this would have eradicated a huge chunk (six sea miles) of the original route travelled by the Heroes which we would live to regret, so I decided to engage the 'Robert The Bruce' theory, and like his persistent spider, 'If at first you don't succeed, try, try again'. It was imperative that we should succeed in order to achieve our objective because ultimately, that's why we were there. This time we decided to utilise all our endeavour and determination, coupled with every ounce of energy we could muster. Pushing off sideways, away from the rocky bank, we adopted a position slightly further offshore. Paddling to the end, we studied the monstrous sight of millions of tons of rushing water, and our ears absorbed the loud roaring sound that it was creating. "Let's go for it!" I shouted, and hurling ourselves headlong into the torrent, heads down, totally focused, with no distractions, we frantically paddled into the pouring cascade. We seemed to be held on the edge of a twelve inch, smooth 'step' of water, indeed the bows were raised clear of the surface. I would describe it as the canoe equivalent of a wheelie! Each stroke of the paddle took so much strength that it felt as 'though we were lifting the boat and its contents up out of the water. Tenaciously, we kept going, paddling and paddling, every stroke dipping into the water with perfect synchronisation, maximising the forward thrusting effect. Physically we heaved, and mentally we willed the Sardine forward until we were almost spent, and then, almost at the point where it didn't seem humanly possible for us to continue, we began to realise that we were making headway. "Don't stop! Don't stop!" I blurted, between dry throated gasps for air. Too scared to ease up, fiercely we kept paddling until we were convinced, and totally sure that we were free from the grasping torrent. Now we were on the right side of the island and on the correct course.

A PEACEFUL HAVEN

Completely whacked, soaked in sweat from the arduous exertion, but with a sense of great achievement throbbing through our veins at getting our canoe and worldly goods back on course, we dropped our paddles on to the deck, hung our lifeless arms by our sides, hands dangling in the lukewarm water, and crumpled down into our seats, inhaling loudly in the hot thin air for oxygen. With the continuous rushing sound of the water gradually mellowing with distance behind us, the Sardine seemed to instinctively, unaided, drift calmly into a small welcoming cove. I grabbed hold of a tuft of grass on the two foot high, vertical gravel bank under a shady tree where we hovered, discussing the dramatic scenario that had just taken place. I hadn't realised that we were capable of consolidating so much strength between us. I think we were both surprised. Again, I was convinced that it just had to be the influence of the Cockleshell Heroes. Somehow they were guiding and charging us with the power and alacrity to follow their route. Having lost so much body fluid, we sipped our water bottles and Sandra broke open the glucose tablets that we hadn't used until now.

CONTRASTS

In complete contrast to our slight discomfort (poor dears, what a tragedy) with the hot, sunny days, Major Hasler and his men had to suffer the freezing cold December nights. It has to be very cold for sea water to freeze, but on some nights, the spray that broke over the Cockles actually froze on their cockpit covers. The dripping water running down their paddle shafts soaked through their woollen mittens, numbing their hands and forming flakes and globules of ice. Like us, they would stop to rest and take Benzedrine tablets. (Note: ours were not Benzedrine!)

WILDLIFE

A very pleasant, gentle paddle followed. The passage between the little Ile de Margeux and the main shoreline was extremely narrow and must have given the Heroes, with regard to remaining undetected, some tense moments. Like weeping willows, large trees on the bank were hanging right over the river with their leafy branches dipping into the water, so we slipped beneath them hugging the bank for shade. The need to keep cool overrode our thoughts of what ghastly objects were lurking below the surface, causing the swirling eddies that we were paddling through. It was a bit like the Orinoco. Throughout this passage, there was an abundance of wildlife, including many herons that looked like tall, lanky, tail coated undertakers. Several times, as we gently approached a tree in which one had perched, it would become unnerved by our close proximity and take flight, amazing us with its gracefulness and terrific wing span. A beaver, disturbed by our presence, with its wet, rat-like furry head held above the water, swam quickly away to its burrow in the bank, or was it a vole or perhaps an otter!? We weren't sure, but it was thrilling to be so close and a privilege to pass through its habitat. The water was noticeably thicker with mud in this area. Almost new moon meant that the tide was running at an even greater rate of knots, but after some precarious wobbly moments, Sandra managed to pass the camera over to a lone ferryman on a small motor craft. With much French bravado, he throttled his boat and sped off in a half circle to our consternation, creating a huge wash. Once in position, with his jolly scruffy mongrel dog stood proud, barking at us from his bow, he snapped a shot for our scrap book. Eventually, six miles later, we reached the end of Ile Verte which changes its name in the middle to Ile du Nord, and then confusingly ends up as Ile Cazeau. We were now at the opposite end of the island that had given us such a challenge earlier on, but this end was much gentler.

A DANGEROUS HIDE

From 6.30am, on the 9th December 1942, Hasler and his chaps began to search for a hiding place. Daylight was threatening, and with tense nerves, they could clearly hear the sounds of traffic and movement from the mainland. Their task was proving very difficult; the island was thickly forested with reeds and undergrowth, and getting ashore seemed impossible. Nearing the southern end, where the island petered out into a sharp point, they came across a small pier. This indicated regular use, but there was a thick wood just a short distance from the bank. Hasler undertook a reccie, but stumbled across an occupied German gun site. Slinking back to Sparks, Laver and Mills who were still rafted up in the reeds, he gave them the bad news and they reluctantly pushed off again. After paddling only a few yards, and with daylight now breaking on them, they scrambled ashore, dragging their canoes to a spot almost at the very tip of the island. By 7.30am they had strewn the camouflage nets over their boats and had begun one of their most tense and uncomfortable days. With only a narrow strip of trees between them and the German gun emplacement, they were pinned down and had no chance of sleeping or cooking. Soaked, cold and caked in thick mud, a comforting cigarette would have been a great morale boost, but because of the close proximity of civilisation and a German gun battery within spitting distance, smoking was completely out of the question, as was relieving themselves. Urination had not been such a problem, but defecation always proved difficult, and for obvious reasons, uncomfortable. However, with the ghastly diet they were obliged to adhere to, this function didn't happen very often. At one point a herd of inquisitive cows formed a circle around them and simultaneously two German soldiers wandered into the field for a smoke. They studied the cows but remarkably did not see the canoes. Several times during their nail biting day, they were buzzed by low flying reconnaissance aircraft, and they could clearly see the pilots sitting in their cockpits, scanning the ground below. Throughout all this, they kept up their resolve, managing to sit motionless and ridged in their uncomfortable wood and canvas prisons. A man walking his dog passed painfully close, but their scent wasn't sniffed, and ultimately their discipline and training saved them from detection. Physically and mentally, they were now seriously feeling the strain. In three nights they had travelled sixty miles, and during three nerve-racking days, they had remained immobile, with their cold wet limbs stiff from fatigue. The mud was freezing on to their uniforms, and every time they moved, they made a cracking noise. Unknown to any of them at the time, MacKinnon and Conway spent the same day hiding on the east side of the same island, just a short distance away.

FROM GIRONDE TO GARONNE

At the furthest most tip of the island, we hung on to an outcrop of long, spindly vegetation that was growing up out of the water. There were some dainty, very pretty little flowers growing on it, and so we picked a few and pressed them between the pages of our log book. Again, this felt like a gentle tribute to those gallant men. Even as we hung on, with the water rushing and swirling by us and under the Sardine, we spent a silent moment in reflection and remembrance. We took a photograph, then letting go, were sent hurtling along, propelled by the racing tide, into a wide expanse of turbulent water like a cork in a bath. It was like the linear equivalent of stepping off a cliff, and like the Cockleshell Heroes, we now left La Gironde and were in La Garonne, and just twelve miles from Bordeaux. La Gironde had divided into two on the other side of Ile Cazeau, becoming La Dordogne, and La Garonne which we now found ourselves at the mercy of. Opposite, and obviously not there at the time of the Operation, we had the pleasant (if you like that sort of thing) view of the enormous oil refinery. We had no idea where we were going to be staying that night, having decided to continue on with the tide. Eventually, it appeared that the tide could be about to turn on us, and the wind was noticeably stronger, so we pulled our hoods up to keep out the comparative chill. In response to the tide and wind change, the water was beginning to get worryingly choppy, so we anxiously began to scan the shoreline in search of a suitable place to stop. We passed a few small protruding grassy banks that in desperation we could have just about squeezed on to, in the hope that we would not have woken up sitting in water. We were sorely tempted to pull over, but the chart clearly showed an inlet or creek nearby, and although we could not make an accurate location identification, we decided to carry on apprehensively against the turning tide to find it. Traversing a slight bend, a green buoy appeared. I glanced at the map and realised that if it was number 65b, it meant that the inlet must be near by. Infused with a new found sudden strength, induced by the thought of rest and recuperation, we paddled like mad out to the centre channel to identify the buoy. As soon as we were close enough to read and realize that yes, it was indeed the correct number, we were paddling back to find the inlet. It became apparent to us that we had overshot it by some hundred metres. This was because the bank was thickly packed with tall reeds, and the inlet ran back on itself. It wasn't until we had passed the entrance that it was possible for us to see it. With the tide in limbo, we were able to backtrack, and once more we felt the relief of slipping gently from the frenetic chaos of the irrational river, into the tangible, contrasting tranquillity of a gentle creek.

OUR FOURTH CAMP
..... A DESPARATE MEASURE

Our relief was soon to turn to anxiety when, upon reaching the predictable obstacle ..... the impenetrable sluice gate ..... we found to our consternation that we were unable to get ashore anywhere. The banks were terribly high and dense with masses of barbed thorn bushes and matted vegetation. We had to get out one way or another, the sun was setting, the water ebbing fast, and we were literally watching it disappear from under us. The thought of spending the night sitting in the Sardine, however attached to it we had become, and however close to the real Operation we wanted to be, was not an attractive one. 'Sod this for a game of soldiers!' was my only contribution. Feeling desperately tired and distraught, with the realisation that all the surrounding farmland was obviously private and occupied, desperate measures were now necessary. Plan 'B' was activated ..... the 'modus operandi!' Until now we hadn't involved or asked for the help of any of the locals. Now that we were in dire straits (not the band!), like Major Hasler when he was forced to approach the French fishermen and women, we were going to have to adopt the same technique. Fifty yards or so back from the sluice gate stood a small, rickety old wooden pier with two equally tatty old wooden rowing boats tied to it. They were in a sorry state ..... paint peeling off and a green ring of slimy mould growing around their waterlines from lack of use. A precarious, long neglected and dilapidated wooden gangway (with the odd split or missing rung for good measure) ran twenty feet over the muddy water to the high, overgrown bank which supported closely knit trees and a tangled mass of rambling bushes. Without getting out, I managed to tie the Sardine to the pier, leaving enough rope for what I gauged to be sufficient length to accommodate the falling tide. I was getting good at judging this now. Sandra spent a few anxious moments whispering through her French dialogue, and then, ripping off the canvas decking, she clambered on to the wobbly structure, and 'minding the gaps', made it to the top of the bank. She briefly glanced back at me, still sitting in the Sardine, and so I gave her the thumbs-up sign, at which she disappeared over the bank and away to the nearby farmhouse. Fortunately, it wasn't long before she returned, accompanied by a beaming young French farmer. It transpired that she had knocked on the farm door, and in perfectly adequate French, was able to convey to him our predicament, at which point he had invited us to camp for the night near his house. He must have wondered at the apparition that had stood there before him, i.e. Sandra, sporting a swarthy complexion, wearing a combat cap and bright yellow life-jacket caked in mud. He helped us carry our plastic container of cooking equipment, tent and overnight belongings past his beautiful sunflower field and on to a grassy area next to the artichokes. Before he left us to it, he pointed to the outside toilet facility, a rude wooden Porto cabin-type structure, and the standpipe, at the top of which was a tap! The setting sun looked magnificent behind the trees as I erected the tent. Near to our camping spot, there was some rusty old farm machinery, so I decided to utilise it as an anvil to straighten our tent pegs. Because of the granite-like ground that we had encountered so far, our tent pegs were, without exaggeration, the shape of horseshoes. I took the rubber mallet and held the first peg down on the cylindrical axel part of a plough-type thing with sharp looking blades and big iron studded wheels. A rain of hard blacksmith blows and it was well on the way to straightness. Suddenly, I had the feeling that someone had placed a red hot iron on the back of my hand. My first reaction was that I had hit my hand with the mallet, but in the half light I saw a hornet hovering on my hand. Instantly I was engulfed by a swarm of them. Dropping the mallet and peg, I ran, arms flailing frantically, into the artichoke field. After a few yards, and with much relief, the hornets petered out to the odd one or two. Like a streak of grey smoke in reverse, they poured back into the tube from whence they came. We never saw them again, we left their home alone, and they left our camp alone. Fortunately Sandra, remaining true to her character, had packed some antihistamine which she then, in 'Florence Nightingale, under the glimmer of our camping lamp' fashion, administered. In the still, dark, warm field, save for the flickering illumination of our lamp, we sat reclining on our propped up mattresses, masticating on lentils and cheese, whilst sipping delicious Blaye red wine. It should be noted that, as a priority and as our equivalent to weapons of mass digestion, we had been sure to pack ..... 'plastic wine goblets, large, two, for the use of' ..... divine!

DAY FIVE: Saturday 17th July
..... THE LAST LEG

Just like the early birds that were singing amongst the trees, we were up at first light, 6.30am, to embrace another beautiful sky, but unfortunately Sandra had suffered a fitful night due to her painful hands (and my hornet sting had throbbed in sympathy). Due to the forward movement of the tide cycle, this was the only morning we were able to set off first thing. In retrospect, it occurred to us that on our first day leaving Port Bloc in the morning, the tide must have still been going out, but because the estuary was so wide at that point and we were literally miles from the channel, floundering in the shallows ineptly trying to get our bearings, we didn't even notice! Whilst the water boiled in the mess tin in preparation for a nice warm wakeup cuppa, I folded and packed the tent away, still wet from the heavy dew. An old Citroen van rumbled up the driveway, past the farmhouse, and stopped near the sunflower field. What we presumed to be the farm hand – a middle-aged, weathered, muddy booted Frenchman – jumped out, wandered over to us, and took a curious look at our incongruous encampment. Some jolly head nodding and hand shaking ensued, and we all understood it to mean, 'Hello, how are you? Good morning, and what on earth are you doing here?' Monsieur Lecroix, our friendly and accommodating farmer, emerged from the house to join us, and Sandra deciphered from his conversation that we were in the area of Parempuyre, and that the tide was high at 9am. Bordeaux, he appeared to be conveying with finger gestures, was only five kilometres away, and therefore we could easily make it in one go. At 7.35am, the farmer and his employee stood on the overgrown bank observing us with amusing disbelief as we completed the wobbly ritual of loading the Sardine. Casting off from the rickety jetty, they began waving endlessly with cries of 'Bon Voyage'. Paddles in one hand, twisting round in our seats, we waved back and responded with, 'Merci beaucoup, au revoir'. Once down the creek we meet our old friend, La Garonne. Unfortunately, the weather began to close in, engulfing us in a heavy wet mist and restricting our visibility to just a few yards. This was worrying for us because, on leaving the farmer's creek, we came dangerously close to a collision with a gigantic tanker. Ironically, our first close encounter with a large vessel happened during our first experience of mist. The new section of the river was very narrow, and through the mist, beyond the banks, we could make out acres of unattractive, sprawling residential and industrial areas. Left behind were all those quaint, sleepy villages and scenic vineyards so elegantly graced with their palatial chateaux. The atmosphere, at that stage, was tangibly different. For so many miles on the river, we had been ostracised from civilisation and had enjoyed the peace and serenity of those practically deserted, welcoming river banks, so it was unnerving getting our first sight of close-up shipping working alongside wharfs. It was almost threatening to suddenly be so near any traffic and to hear the throbbing populace massed on the fringes of Bordeaux. It had been the same for the Cockleshell Heroes at this point, except that their threat was potentially deadly. Expecting to soon reach our goal, we paddled along, feeling very wet, but warm, and pleased with ourselves. Looming right ahead, lazily arching over the river was the enormous Bordeaux road bridge, Le Pont d'Aquitaine. Nearly there! Our elation was short lived as within seconds, like an extravagant magic trick, the wet mist engulfed the bridge and it totally disappeared from our view. It seemed ages paddling through the mist before we caught a glimpse of it again, and even worse, it didn't appear to be any closer. It was obviously bigger, and further away than we had calculated. Not only that, we realised that the farmer's casual estimate of five kilometres to Bordeaux was far out. The way I saw it, having consulted the chart, was that we still had at least half an hour's paddling to do, and our morale went into a dive when Sandra announced that she thought the tide was beginning to turn on us. We both knew that we just had to make it today; we were so close to the Operation Frankton time that, without a word passing between us, instinctively we dipped our paddles in unison and made a mad dash in an attempt to get there. After ten or so minutes, we realised the tide was beating us, and so, whilst Sandra continued to paddle, preventing us from slipping back, I quickly consulted the chart for an inlet or suitable stopping place. Across the river, situated below the large concrete struts of the bridge, we could see the welcoming shape of a floating pontoon with a solitary yacht alongside. With the tide almost at full belt against us, this peace haven was frustratingly out of our reach. Fortunately, corresponding with the chart, I spotted a breach in the bank to our right. It was the entrance to a creek. Will power and pure brawn against tide got us there, and once again we slipped gently up the creek ….. with a paddle ….. to meet yet another sluice gate. With the water dwindling rapidly below the Sardine, revealing the brown stodgy mud banks, we hastily tied up alongside a jigsaw of scrap wood struts, beams and old hardboard, all encrusted in a layer of disgusting mud, and purporting to be a jetty. The adjoining land was disused and littered with the rubble and broken concrete remains of long since derelict factories. There were some youths screaming around on scramble motorbikes nearby, and we could hear some very heavy traffic noise coming from a main road. With all this in mind, Sandra nimbly climbed up on to the slippery planks, whilst I repositioned the Sardine on the far side of the pier, out of sight, secured with the padlock and chain. In that short space of time, the water had quickly receded as 'though someone had pulled the plug out, and Sandra was stressing as to how I would mount the now exposed ten foot high muddy jetty. I passed up the paddles and some supplies for the day, and then employed my Army obstacle course techniques to haul myself up from the canoe. We hid the paddles and our rubber shoes in the undergrowth, ate a few nuts and raisins, togged up, and headed off along the ragged river bank towards the sound of the traffic.

DEMORALISED

Photograph: U boat pens

Rain drizzled down upon us as we trudged along the seemingly endless, rubbish strewn, wet and sandy hard shoulder of the busy main road. An endless torrent of traffic thundered past, showering us with filthy spray, leaving us in the wake of its slipstream. My tiredness began to take over, and my patience and resolve began to falter. In this grey, wet, dirty place, it all seemed so futile and pointless, and it felt so far from home and everything that we were accustomed to. My subconscious mind kept asking me, 'What are we doing, slogging our tired bodies along this miserable road? Nobody knows we're here, so what's the point? What are we trying to prove? Why don't we just hail a taxi and go home?' Our hopes were momentarily raised when we came across a bus shelter. However, on reading the timetable, it transpired that the buses didn't run that far from town on a Saturday. Eventually, we found ourselves walking beneath the vast structure of the towering Pont d'Aquitaine where it straddled the shoreline road before joining the main highway. We continued on into Bordeaux via the commercial quays which we judged to be about three miles. Our spirits were raised once again when we discovered the swing bridge lock gates at the entrance to the commercial basins. Built of thick steel and encrusted with thousands of rivets, they were designed to swing open and allow ships in and out. Dominating the second of the two basins was a formidable complex of concrete U boat pens. They had been built by the Germans during the war. Like a set from a James Bond film, we half expected to see Mr Nasty Rogue person appear with his evil, oily smile, announcing a dastardly plan to conquer the planet. In reality, that was just what Hitler and his henchmen had tried to achieve. It was there that we had intended to finish our trip, mooring the Sardine in the marina area, but it was not to be. Several false leads later, having been misdirected (but not deliberately) by the citizens and fellow English tourists in the centre of Bordeaux, we finally located the elusive Tourist Office, only to be told that the Basins were closed, as was the Base Sous-Marine museum as it was not currently housing an exhibition . Whatever, it didn't really matter to us because at last we were in the centre of Bordeaux, the sun had come out, our clothes were beginning to dry, and that comforting combination made us feel much happier. Hand-in-hand, we ambled through La Place des Quinconces, the grand square that lay just off the embankment on which once stood a chateau. We wandered on past an ornate, prestigious stone sculptured monument marking the defeat of the English in 1814, depicting bare breasted muscular women wearing steel helmets, holding shields and swords, smiting the foe that lay sprawled beneath their sandaled feet Bordering the square, several avenues of trees formed a leafy roof over the busy central tram terminal. Swish bullet nosed trams with tinted windows swept in and out, ferrying tourists and locals through the tracked arteries of the city. Just off the vast square, we lounged in our steaming clothes in the comfortable and busy ambience of 'Le Regent Café'. Chomping on tasty toasted cheese sandwiches, and downing large luxurious glasses of French beer, we observed the patrons and absorbed the friendly atmosphere, whilst bringing up-to-date our soggy log books. As is customary in France, we participated in the offer of two free glasses of water. Feeling a little more human, but still physically aching, we walked the three miles back to the Sardine. It rained on us all the way back, and Sandra suffered a nasty dose of colic. The rain persisted throughout the reloading and relaunching antics, but ceased as soon as we took advantage of a narrow channel of water, sufficient for us to glide back into the main stream of La Garonne.

ALMOST SUNK

Photograph: Pont d'Aquitaine

The tide carried us at a good pace, and we felt in high spirits as we accurately crossed the river at an obtuse angle, passing under the impressive expanse of Le Pont d'Aquitaine suspension bridge, at last arriving at the floating pontoon situated a few hundred yards further. Nervously, we manoeuvred ourselves up against the pontoon, astern of a beautifully varnished, traditionally styled wooden sailing yacht. This action proved to be a feat of our wits and strength against the rushing tide's determination to sweep us, Sardine and all, under the whole contraption. With our arms stretched up, hanging on with our bare hands (like two dislodged tightrope walkers) to their stern mooring rope, and with the tide rushing noisily, gurgling under our hull, we chatted to the charming late middle-aged Dutch couple on board the yacht. They were amazed to hear a short account of our journey, and informed us that the tide should be turning around 8-8.30pm. We didn't contradict them as we welcomed their help, but our hands-on experience told us that it would be more like 9.30-10pm, and as it turned out, we were correct. They also informed us that the mooring was free and much safer than any of the other locations in the area. It had a substantial aluminium gangway with wooden decking leading up to the top of the river bank with a secure metal gate. We explained that we had to complete our journey by paddling the mile or so to the Bordeaux quays, and that we would return thereafter to moor alongside. The second we let go of the rope, we were swept forward and almost underneath the sloping stern of the yacht. An anxious few seconds ensued as we tried frantically to turn the Sardine away from the pontoon and past the yacht. For a brief agonising moment, the stern of the Sardine slipped round, and the weight of the current began to push our starboard side down under the water until the brown torrent was almost sweeping over our deck. I could see us being dragged broadside, smashed into the yacht's large wooden rudder and swept under its hull. Miraculously, although I'm not sure what action we adopted with the paddles, we recovered control (with the Heroes' help!?), sliding down the side of the yacht and out into the river. To me it felt like the most perilous moment of the trip I really thought we were going to be sucked under their boat. To lose everything, including our lives, at that stage of our expedition would have been tragic. It took a few minutes for me to compose myself afterwards.

COCKLESHELLS LAST NIGHT

On the night of 10th December 1942 at around ten o'clock, Major Hasler, Sparks, Laver and Mills arrived in this same area and spotted their targets. Their toil and loss of comrades were about to be rewarded. Their fatigue evaporated, being replaced by the thrill of anticipation. They ducked their heads and slipped under a pontoon pier similar to the one that we had encountered. However, their elation was tinged with worry as, unlike in England where important industrial sites were blacked out against air raids, the target ships and the surrounding port were bathed in light, and they could clearly hear the cranes and men working on the docks. Fortunately they located several small runnels of water that penetrated the thick reed beds lining the western bank. Picking one, they slipped amongst the reeds in just a few inches of water and pushed their canoes in as far as possible. Cosily they rafted up, side-by-side, around eleven o'clock. It was a cloudy night with occasional rain. Remaining in their canoes, the tide ebbed and they settled on to the mud. For the whole night and all the next day they remained motionless, sitting in their canoes. It was an excellent hide with the rushes towering up over their heads at least nine feet or so. Occasionally they were able to gently stand up, unobserved in their canoes, have a stretch, and peer through the reeds at their prey moored on the opposite bank. There were some good-sized ships opposite, making it all feel worthwhile, and they couldn't wait to get a crack at them. Just beyond their hide in the dense reeds lay a big built-up area of commercial and domestic occupation. During the day it was noisy and swarming with people and traffic, not to mention the Germans and Vichy police. They were on the verge of completing their mission, and this cheeky little party of defiant soldiers was about to give the German high command a shaking to the core. All the noise and activity enabled them to smoke and talk in whispers. Hasler planned that the two canoes would reach the target area an hour before high water, enabling them to drift through the docks on the last of the flood tide. In theory, after placing their limpet mines on the targets, they would drift back on the first ebb. There was a young moon and the sky was clear, not good for crossing the river under German noses, so leaving it until 9.10pm, they crossed the harbour towards the targets. Hasler had elected to work along the western bank of the main docks of Bordeaux, some three miles ahead, and gave Laver and Mills orders to search the eastern dock. If they found nothing there, they were to return and attack the vessels moored opposite their last hide at Bassens South, the ones that they had been gloating over. During the day, they rearranged their gear so that all the escape materials were in two convenient bags. After the mission, they were to paddle downstream with the ebb until the tide turned, or it became daylight. They were then to scuttle their canoes and make their escape on the eastern bank. In the late evening, during the last hour before setting off into the attack, they set the fuses fizzing on the sixteen limpet mines. They turned the thumbscrew of each fuse until a faint 'click' told that the glass of the ampoule of liquid acetone inside the fuse had been broken. The washer holding back the striker pin would slowly dissolve, and in nine hours time, the firing pin would spring forward and hit the detonator. The mines were also fitted with a secondary sympathetic fuse to eradicate the possibility of the first explosion knocking the others off, only to explode on the river bed. After eating their last meal, the four attackers blackened their faces, and hid the luminous compasses.

THE ATTACK

Both crews shook hands and wished each other good luck before sliding the canoes through the mud, and silently paddling away to work as two independent parties. Weather conditions were not in their favour, there was no rain to deaden the sound of their paddles, and there was a cloudless starry sky. To compound it all, the glaring port and factory lights made the possibility of detection greater. After an hour and a half of paddling, Hasler and Sparks spotted a long line of brightly lit ships moored alongside the quays on the west bank. Passing the entrance to the locks, they swept out from the right bank and back in a half moon to avoid the lights illuminating the basins. Sweeping out gave them the added opportunity of identifying target ships because once under their steep towering sides, there was no way of knowing whether they were worth attacking. Moving down on to the targets, they passed a tanker but ignored it, and then a passenger ship which they also left alone. Next they came alongside a large cargo ship with a tanker moored alongside and considered them for later, if there were any limpet mines left. Just a few yards ahead, they were under a perfect target, a large cargo ship. Already they could feel the tide going out so now speed was of the essence. Their hard learned, team honed precision drills went like clockwork. Hiding in the shadows that were cast by the enemy vessels, Sparks pulled back his canvas cockpit cover, as did Hasler, to reveal the eight fizzing limpet mines, magnetic hold fast, and the six foot long folding, articulated placing rod. Gingerly anchoring themselves against the gigantic looming hulls, they systematically attached the mines below the waterline of the cargo ship and the German sperrbrecher naval vessel. It was a delicate, slow and laborious task, and by the time they had finished, the tide was so fast against them that it would prove impossible to reach any more of the ships. All was not yet lost ..... they turned and went back with the current until they reached the previous cargo ship with the tanker rafted alongside. Voices and music reverberating from crews' quarters could faintly be heard through the thick steel hulls, and having their camouflaged hoods up turned out to be good protection against the discharging water and sewage that spewed out and drenched them from time-to-time. During a spine chilling moment, a sentry peered over the side of a ship and actually shone his torch down on them. With no option but to sit frozen and motionless in the canoe, they held their breath and waited for a machine gun to open up on them. As they drifted alongside the ship, the guard followed them, his torch beam burning into their exposed backs. Eventually they drifted under the bows of the ship, below the anchor, and out of the guard's sight. Hasler handed the magnetic holdfast device to Sparks who gingerly and silently rolled it on to the ship, thus preventing them from drifting out into the open. Unbelievably, after ten minutes that seemed like hours, the torch went out, and the sentry, happy that they were flotsam or jetsam, walked casually away, clanking across the deck. Their task was now to relieve themselves of the remaining limpet mines before being swept away by the gathering force of the ebb tide. They slid the canoe between two rafted ships but quickly became trapped as the current forced the ships together. Hearing the brittle wooden frame of the canoe splitting under the vice-like pressure of the ships, it seemed inevitable that they would be crushed between the monstrous steel bulkheads. They considered setting off the mines rather than be defeated at this crucial stage. However, before they could implement such self-sacrificing act of heroism, the two ships moved slowly apart, releasing them. Having planted the remaining limpets to the stern of the merchantman and tanker, Major Hasler twisted round and shook Sparks' hand. They both laughed freely for the first time in hours and felt a reckless sense of devil-may-care. The job was done, and their canoe was markedly lighter without the limpets. Treating the enemy with contempt, they boldly paddled out to the centre channel, and with the fast tide behind them, made hard their escape. Heading full pelt in the direction of Blaye, Major Hasler thought of Laver and Mills, and hoped that they had experienced as much success finding their prey. As it transpired, whilst Hasler and Sparks were taking a short breather in the channel just past the Ile de Cazeau, the sound of splashing paddles came out of the mist. It was Laver and Mills who reported that they had in fact attached their deadly surprises on the two large ships at Bassens South. As we know, after scuttling 'Catfish' and 'Crayfish' at Blaye, Hasler and Sparks split with their comrades and started their gruelling 1,400 mile overland escape on foot, without proper food or clothing, in the depths of winter.

OUR TRIUMPHANT ARRIVAL

Having recovered from the fracas with the rear end of the Dutch yacht, we paddled on with the roaring choppy tide. Like the Cockleshell Heroes, we swiftly passed the entrance to the basins, but without having to avoid any lights or German sentries, and on towards our target. Within a few minutes, with emotion welling up inside us, we cast our excited and tear blurred eyes on the majestic riverside city of Bordeaux. We'd made it! ..... mission accomplished ..... more than 100 kilometres in five days, one day ahead of schedule ..... but it was a strange and solitary elation. The quayside was bustling with walkers, joggers, inline skaters, cyclists, shoppers and humming traffic, yet we were the only two in Bordeaux aware of our mission. If we hadn't been sat in tandem in the Sardine, I'm sure we would have embraced. On cue, as 'though heralding our arrival, a rock-n-roll band blared out from a shed on the opposite bank. With our favourite style of music echoing across the river to the city, we graciously adopted this as our reception party. Indeed, people cheerfully waved to us from the busy bank, and fancifully, we imagined the Cockleshell Heroes mingling amongst them, acknowledging our tribute to their courage and sacrifice for freedom. The music was so relevant as we have our own rock-n-roll band, and we felt justly grand paddling along to the rocking rhythms, revelling in our sense of achievement. From our mid-river, Sardine perspective, it was a beautiful gracious city with fine traditional architecture, graced with trees and large ornate stately buildings. Tied up alongside the quay, and creating an authentic warlike atmosphere, stood a grey imposing French battleship (the Croiseur Colbert). It made us feel like a real attacking force. Being the eve of the new moon, Sandra was concerned that the ferocious spring tide would wash us beneath the old Pont de Pierre that spanned the far end of the city, so we hove-to out of the current in a small sheltered inlet below a concrete wharf structure, waiting the half hour or so for the tide to turn, before making our way back to the pontoon. The bridge had the appearance of an old Roman viaduct supported by a series of stone arches. Twenty feet above us, people were leisurely perambulating and enjoying their fitness hobbies. From time-to-time, passers-by hung over the metal railing and peered curiously down at us bobbing about as we sat eating our chocolate peanuts from a plastic container. A busy beaver (vole? otter?) swam past unperturbed, and scurried on to his grassy embankment, eventually disappearing beneath the superstructure of the wharf. A well dressed middle-aged couple expressed their concern for us being in such a small craft in such a perilous river, explaining that the tides were very dangerous, but nevertheless wished us good luck. The woman spoke fluent English but was dumbstruck on hearing that we had voyaged all the way from Pointe de Grave. 'In that!?' she exclaimed, throwing her French gesticulating arms up in horror, trying to explain it to her husband. They were shortly followed by a nutter, clad in latex cycling gear, and wearing one of those stupid looking aerodynamic cycling helmets that made him appear like a demented moth. He also spoke good English but became very heated, and began blurting out abuse such as, 'You shouldn't be in the water, it's dangerous with shipping, what do you think you're doing in there, this isn't a boating lake! People have drowned in the Garonne!' Not prepared to take any more of his crazy rantings, we battened down the canvas decking and pushed off towards mid channel and back up river in the direction of the floating pontoon where the Dutch people were moored. The tide still hadn't quite turned, so to begin with we were going against its final thrusts, dodging the now customary floating debris. It was 9pm and we endured a hard forty five minute paddle back to the little marina trying to beat the dark, and all the way we were haunted by that village idiot's ravings. Our triumphant mood had temporarily been spoilt, and for the first time on our trip, we were conscious of our vulnerability. The water became choppy, the sky sinister with impending thundery clouds looming in the cool dusky evening, and the wind whipped up a cold stinging spray against our faces. It wasn't the reception we had expected

..... there were no accolades, no praise for what we believed we had achieved, just a bunch of derogatory comments from a stupid busybody, leaving our thoughts and emotions in turmoil.

Not a word was spoken between us until we finally reached the pontoon at 9.45pm and relative safety. A few wobbly moments fighting for the last time with the Garonne's ebbing current as we tied up, and it was with a great sense of relief that we finally found ourselves standing on the floating pontoon at the Lormont Club de Voile, being welcomed by the Dutch couple who had been looking out for us in the 'Cacao' river, as they said it was nicknamed! They confessed to us that they had been slightly worried by our late return, and further compounded our new misery by adding that our canoe seemed so small to be in such a big and unpredictable river. They gave us the number of the Club's security guard in case the gate was locked when we returned, and then retired to their classically rigged yacht on the opposite side of the pontoon, leaving us to unpack from the Sardine whatever we could manage to carry. Lumbering up the gangway with our belongings, we stopped at the gate and glanced down one last time at the Sardine. Left to its fate, it sat there looking very small, forlorn and fragile all alone in the dark, apart from the towering pontoon and two other yachts. It had proved to be a sturdy, faithful, and most reliable friend and companion that had kept us both safe and had completed the task most admirably. The Sardine had a blemish free record, served us well, and had been our home and store for the whole eventful and enjoyable journey. The bow nodded up and down on the rippling water and seemed to be saying, 'Fare thee well', or maybe, 'Au revoir'.

CIVILISATION – 'B & B'

The area behind the Lormont Club de Voile was rather ragged and residential. It had no hotel or any other obvious sign of accommodation available, but there were a couple of restaurants and café bars. Although it was late, I felt relaxed and confident that we would be spending the night in a proper bed! Looking like two, muddy, damp itinerant travellers, we selected a café and tramped inside. A gregarious, bleached blond, middle-aged landlady, her face adorned with more than her fair share of colourful cosmetics, poured us a couple of beers. Sandra was surprised to hear familiar Arabic music playing (being a belly dancer in 'real life'), but being both exhausted and inappropriately dressed, she could not even manage the slightest of undulations. Instead, she conversed in French and discovered there was a hotel, but it was too far to walk, especially with all our clobber. The madame epitomised the helpful and obliging French that we had so far encountered and, unprompted, 'phoned for a taxi. There was a noisy interchange of conversation, as it transpired that the taxi driver had quoted twenty five euros. "Trop cher, trop cher!" she rightly exclaimed. To our surprise, she scooped up her jacket and car keys, and a thirty minute car drive later (which incorporated a couple of wrong turns and a backing out of a one way system), we were alighting in the forecourt of the 'B & B Hotel'. She flatly refused any monetary remuneration for her trouble, but I did manage to thrust all my pocket change into her hand before she sped off into the night. Alone, on a dark drizzling night, loaded down with baggage, we found ourselves outside the floodlit accommodation, facing an automatic booking-in contraption. Self-confessed computer dinosaurs that we are, we ineptly prodded at the screen of the computerised receptionist, and after a couple of failures and crackly conversation with a disembodied voice from the central office, we successfully programmed it to give us a double room for one night, reserve breakfast for two, and print out our receipt with a personal pin number. Using the pin number on the door key pad miraculously gained us entrance to our room. It was a ten by ten clean, serviceable, uniform, but comfortable cell in a stark, but functional block of identical barrack-like apartments. There was a TV with remote control on a coiled wire, towels and en suite bathroom. Without undressing, apart from my boots, I stepped fully clothed into the exhilarating hot water jets of the shower. Using the soap dispenser, and to Sandra's amusement, I washed my clothes and peeled them off gradually until my garments and I were completely clean and revived. This was our first proper wash since Blaye. Soaking up the relative luxury, we lay warm, glowing and comfortable on the bed, drinking our wine and laughing at a French farce on the television. It was so stereotyped with all the hallmarks and characters of a British farce that we didn't need any command of the language to recognise and understand the plot. During the night, there was a tremendous storm, with torrential rain, bright flashes of lightning and explosive bangs of thunder. Of course, this was the night that coincided with the ships being blown up! How the Sardine was faring concerned us. Although I had secured the canvas decking and covered the two round waist holes with bin liners, there was no way that all that rain could be held at bay. Perhaps it had sunk, spilling the remains of our belongings into the river, down to Davy Jones' locker; anyway, there was no reason for us to worry as there was nothing we could do about it.

Sunday 18th July

Nine o'clock, and we were in the communal dining room, tucking into our inclusive and most adequate, take-as-much-as-you-like, cooked breakfast. Amusingly, the instant scrambled egg was bright yellow in colour, but quite palatable, and the processed bacon, although we didn't sample it, came in identical matching rectangular strips, with squared off ends. Apart from the correct colour and smell, there was no resemblance to anything from a pig. Sandra surreptitiously smuggled some extra croissants into a serviette for later, and we stoked ourselves with gallons of tea and coffee. Over breakfast, we had changed our original plan to see Bordeaux on the Sunday, and decided that we should return to Pointe de Grave on the train, collect the car, travel back to Bordeaux, and then pay a visit to the 'Centre Jean Moulin' French Resistance museum. Leisurely, like our wet clothes, we hung around in our room until the allotted turning out time of midday. Wearing our slightly damp things, but feeling unperturbed in the warm weather, we happily boarded a Bordeaux bound tram that conveniently terminated just a couple of hundred yards down the road from the 'B & B Hotel'. That simple operation wasn't without its problems. Unbelievably, we saw a tram leave the platform in front of our very eyes as we struggled with our brain cells and the automatic ticket machine, even 'though it had an English translation. Aware of our dilemma, a kindly French lady came to our aid, and within seconds, produced two one-way tickets to Bordeaux town centre. The central railway station was seething with passengers, and by a million-to-one chance, we literally bumped into the Dutch couple. They were frantically 'doing the city', but before jumping on to a tram, they were able to reassure us that the Sardine, although full of water from the storm, was still afloat. The queues for the ticket booths were hopelessly endless, like undulating snakes, so we stupidly opted for the ticket machine. As our train (the last that day) was standing at the platform ready to leave in precisely two minutes, drastic action was called for, so we left the wretched machine, still arrogantly flashing some undecipherable command, and ran past the mile long ticket queue before leaping from the platform, ticketless, on to the train, hoping that we wouldn't be arrested. It was the oldest, rustiest dented piece of scrap metal in the station, and against all the other sleek, state-of-the-art intercity models on the other tracks, it resembled an antique. We were convinced that it must have been used by some of the Cockleshell Heroes during their escape, and feeling guilty for not having purchased any tickets, we compared our predicament to their evasion from capture, and imagined a German guard might suddenly appear and ask for our identification. Instead, an attractive young female ticket inspector, wearing a man's peaked cap, approached us via the rolling aisle and without any qualms or question, took our money and legalised us with tickets.

BORDEAUX BACK TO POINTE DE GRAVE

Gazing inquisitively out of the brownish, age-stained carriage windows, we sat on the threadbare, but comfortable, forward facing double seat, whilst the train hurtled along at bullet velocity, rattling and screeching at breakneck speed, flinging us past the grimy, graffiti scrawled suburbs and out into the serene countryside. At times we caught a nostalgic view of La Gironde, and being elevated in the carriage, we could observe a good panoramic view over the rolling vineyards, including certain landmarks that we had visually clung to from the Sardine. Remarkably, at 3.15pm, brakes grinding us to a halt, the train stopped right opposite the ferry terminal car park at Pointe de Grave ....., what a relief to find our Mondeo still parked where we had left it six days earlier, safe and sound, and how dramatically the atmosphere had changed. The sun was shining gloriously, and the port and ferry areas were buzzing with cyclists, cars, and Sunday tourists. Pleased as Punch and Judy, Sandra and I sat under a parasol on the veranda of a small wooden café and ordered two portions of frites with two cold beers for our celebration meal. Consuming them with relish, whilst the car ferries came and went amongst all the usual holiday port activity, we pondered profoundly and philosophically over the past five days. Was it really a daring adventure ..... or were we just plain mad!? No other canoes or pleasure boats had we seen during the whole trip. The tides had been extremely strong, and the weather had changed quickly and often. The spirits of the Cockleshell Heroes had remained with us, guided us, and protected us. All the French people that we had encountered were relaxed, amiable, and without exception, most helpful. To our surprise, in the rural areas, it was most unusual to find anyone with even a dash of English, they either spoke it well, or not at all, there was no happy medium, and that included the younger generation. Overall, we decided that life was a lot less complicated in the parts of France that we had visited, and much better organised.

Monday 19th July

Photograph: At Memorial, Pointe aux Oiseaux

Having canoed, trammed and trained down and up the Gironde, we now rode in our hot, sticky car, hugging the river bank as much as the winding road would allow. Leaving the main tarmac road at Pointe aux Oiseaux, we drove carefully for a few miles along the gravel cart track that ran along the top of the dyke. Our aim was to locate the exact spot that Hasler, Sparks, Laver and Mills came ashore after their first night. Eventually, the track became so rough and unkempt that we decided, before losing the exhaust pipe, we would have to concede defeat and locate the main road. However, by chance, we happened to stumble across a wooden chalet-type café, and with a simultaneous chorus of 'tea!' we pulled into its deserted car park. Following a brief investigation, peering through closed shutters, twisting handles and knocking on doors, we came to the conclusion that it was 'ferme!' Resigned to no refreshment, we sat on the dyke wall. Although familiar to us, it seemed strange to be viewing the river from the land, and feeling an affinity, we had an overwhelming urge to be back on it. Sandra, still gasping for a cuppa, returned to the car, and I wandered curiously over to a new looking, seven foot tall, red brick pillar. To my jaw dropping astonishment, it was a recently erected memorial to commemorate the landing of the Cockleshell Heroes at that very spot. Sandra and I scrutinised all the written information, and gazed wide-eyed at the black and white photographs of the actual men whom we had been commemorating. For us that was an elevating and emotional moment. It was the first tangible endorsement that they really had been here, and that we were standing in the exact same place where they had hidden from the enemy on that cold winter's day in December 1942. Were we drawn there!? ..... undoubtedly! What we had done suddenly drew breath and came to life. A car drove into the car park, and the occupants, like us, were disappointed to find the café closed, but they did obligingly take a photograph of Sandra and myself next to the monument. This poignant photograph later appeared in our local Echo, along with a follow up article. Still hugging the coast as much as possible, our next stop was the ferry dock opposite Blaye. With the tide out, we wondered how on earth we managed to round the top of Ile Verte in the racing current, as a stone wall sea defence lay exposed ..... hence, like spawning salmon, it had felt like we were paddling up hill.

RETURN TO BORDEAUX

On reaching humid Bordeaux, we found navigating our way around tributaries of roads and through busy traffic a flustering task, but eventually we managed to locate the Lormont Club de Voile and were relieved to see the Sardine still tied up to the pontoon. It was around 7pm when we finally pulled it out of the water. The rain from the storm had almost filled it which was ironic considering that throughout the trip, we never once capsized or took on a serious amount of water. We rolled it to eject the rainwater, and salvaged all the sodden things that had been left inside, and stood on the jetty squeezing greeny-blue dye from our faithful mattresses. I unwrapped my bundle of tools, pliers, screwdriver, Stanley knife, etc, to find them red with fresh rust. Once the Sardine was strapped on to the roof rack, and the car packed, we gladly accepted the kind offer of a supper consisting of bread, cheese and wine on board the Dutch couple's yacht, 'Johanna'. The wine flowed freely as we exchanged boating tales. Hans and Phyllis were in awe of our experience, but cursed as a river ferry sent a huge wash crashing their precious boat against the pontoon, and even worse, spilling our wine. They told us how they had spent three dry months sailing from Holland, through the French canals, to Bordeaux, and were now awaiting the arrival of Hans' friend to crew the boat down river and back to Holland. Phyllis thought it was too dangerous and was flying back. Suddenly the tarpaulin we were sitting beneath was being pelted by another torrential thunderstorm, breaking the sultry atmosphere.

'CENTRE JEAN MOULIN' MUSEUM

After another comfortable night at the 'B & B Hotel', we enjoyed a delightful and informative horse drawn carriage ride around the city of Bordeaux (driven by a female driver, resplendent in traditional, brown ankle length skirt and full livery, complete with top hat). Inquisitively, we then climbed the steps to the entrance of 'Centre Jean Moulin' museum and walked inside. Most of the exhibits and artefacts represented the heroic exploits carried out by the brave people of the Resistance. Mounted on an easel and very prominently situated in the main hall, we found a wooden memorial plaque to the men of Operation Frankton. Aware of our interest, the curator directed us upstairs to the 'secretariat' who welcomed us to look at all their documentation on the subject. Naturally for us, being able to browse through the overwhelming volume of exclusive documents, photographs, and details of the Operation, was a wonderful opportunity. Sandra did well with her French and managed to explain what we had done. We gave the intrigued administrator our newspaper article featuring the photograph of us in the Sardine, and in return, she kindly spent ages photocopying every single page of the Operation Frankton file. As we were leaving the Records Office with our bundle of photocopies and several 'merci beaucoups', she was trying to tell us about something downstairs, but we couldn't understand what it was. In frustration, she beckoned us to follow her down the stairs to the basement. By that time, we thought we had seen and experienced everything we possibly could in connection with the Cockleshell Heroes, and would have returned home quite contented. How wrong we were … the lady ushered us through an old door, and the three of us shuffled into a dark, dank store room. When the light came on, Sandra and I were greeted with the most amazing sight, the 'piece de resistance' and the real culmination of our journey. Right there in front of us, supported upon two wooden trestles, was a magnificent, exact replica of a Cockleshell Mark II. The Holy Grail!

HOMEWARD BOUND (ESCAPE) FOR HASLER AND SPARKS

For Major Hasler and Bill Sparks, the journey home (or rather the escape whilst avoiding detection and certain death) was long (almost three months), dangerous, bitterly cold, wet, and extremely arduous. With the help of the dubious French Resistance and the reluctant Spanish, the journey took them from Blaye to Lyons, down to Marseilles, through the Pyrenees, Barcelona, Madrid, Gibraltar, and finally after covering 1,400 miles, home to England. Meanwhile, back home, all the families of the men involved were issued with telegrams to the effect that they were 'missing'. It wasn't until the end of February that a coded message from Hasler got through to say that he and Sparks were still alive. Hasler and Sparks were intellectually and socially incompatible, and so the long time they spent in very close proximity to each other on the escape was awkward and uncomfortable. They were from different class backgrounds and had nothing in common to talk about. Bill summed it up to me simplistically by saying, with his characteristically infectious laugh, "He (Hasler) liked cricket, and I preferred football ..... we just didn't speak!"

HOMEWARD BOUND FOR US

Photograph: Rose Garden and Plaque

We arrived at the Cherbourg docks only to discover that we had infuriatingly missed the dammed ferry back to Poole, not by a few minutes, but by twenty three hours! We had even camped nearby in the Municipal campsite and awoken early, hoping to be one of the first in the queue, but instead found ourselves the only car in a deserted ferry terminal. On checking our ticket, we were aghast to discover the wrong date had been booked, Furthermore, that particular morning, the ferry had left an hour early. Because we had a very important business commitment the same evening, we ended up having to bite the bullet and take the very next available ferry. This unwanted and unplanned deviation entailed buying another ticket, sailing to Portsmouth, and from there, driving home to Poole. It was as 'though we were destined to end up in exactly the same place that the Heroes had begun their mission sixty years earlier. We just couldn't resist the opportunity of revisiting Canoe Lake and the Rose Garden. We positioned the car, crowned with the Sardine and adorned with mud from the Gironde, neatly in front of the lake, and asked a passer-by to take our photograph. Looking very pleased with ourselves, the gentleman seemed intrigued, so we briefly told our story much to his astonishment and genuine interest. Illegally, we then drove across the pavement and on to the narrow tarmac garden path, delicately negotiating our way amongst the astonished strolling people. To allow us passage, and to prevent them being run over by us, they were forced to press their backs into the hedges and flower beds. Gingerly, we drove on, past the tennis club, eventually arriving at the Rose Garden. Hastily, before the park police arrived to exact their wroth upon us, we posed the car, Sardine aloft, alongside the gate bearing the commemorative plaque, and swiftly snapped a few more shots for the record. Relieved and happy to have successfully completed our mission, we left Portsmouth behind us, and drove contentedly home to Poole.

RANK INFLUENCE AND PERKS

Major Hasler being an officer and a gentleman! was able to return to England from Madrid more swiftly and elegantly than Sparks. Because of his certain features, Major Hasler was able to wine and dine with distinguished personnel and be entertained by flamenco dancers, whilst poor Sparks, 'because of his certain features', was forced to languish, claustrophobically, in hiding. Not only that, Sparks, after being left behind by Hasler in Madrid, trudged on to Gibraltar, only to suffer the indignity and humiliation (after all he had endured for his country) of being arrested as a spy by the British Military Police, and from there was transported back to England in close custody. As Bill jovially put it to me, "Major Hasler got home first because he was seen as 'utmost priority', and I was seen as 'less of a priority'." Bill Sparks, the jolly cockney and unquestionable war hero, gave the slime-bag MP's the slip at Euston Station in London, and went merrily home to see his family who, thanks to the unsympathetic authorities and their system, believed that he was no more. A few days later, when he was ready, he voluntarily returned to face the music, and even then, it was some time before the chair bound, boneheaded bureaucrats finally believed he was who he claimed to be.

THE OUTCOME OF THE RAID

The limpet mines caused much structural damage to the target ships, and the tiresome job of repairing and removing the sunken vessels from the harbour was labour intensive and time consuming. Shock, disbelief and consternation reverberated through to the complacent German upper echelons. When the Germans eventually discovered how the attack had been done, they couldn't believe it. They couldn't conceive that canoeists would penetrate and traverse such a long busy river right under their noses. Adolf Hitler went into a rage when he learned of the heavy damage caused to the ships in Bordeaux and demanded, in his characteristic foaming at the mouth, desk thumping rant, that more resources be devoted to patrols onshore and to boats in the estuary. His commanders on the ground were immediately sent into a fearful frenzy of action, increasing observation to intensify and aid detection in order to prevent any such attack happening again, knowing that if it did, heads would roll.

Three cargo ships, a tanker and a Sperrbrecher were attacked, damaged and sunk: The Tannenfels, The Alabama, The Portland, one tanker and The Dresden.

We had the pivilege of being invited as guests on Sandi Toksvig's 'Excess Baggage' on BBC Radio 4. During the interview, Sandi asked, "Apparently Sir Winston Churchill said that Operation Frankton shortened the War by six months. Do you think that's true?" I replied, "If anyone knew what was going on, then he did, and I believe it shocked the enemy that canoes could penetrate so far inland causing such damage, ultimately forcing the Germans to use vital resources to defend land and sea."

JUST REWARDS

After the Operation, and prompted by Lord Louis Mountbatten, Hasler was given the DSO with brevet majority and was promoted to Lieutenant-Colonel.

For his exceptional valour in Operation Frankton, Bill Sparks was awarded the Distinguished Service Medal, presented personally to him by King George V1.

Laver and Mills were recommended for the DSM, but because only the VC can be awarded posthumously, they were simply and meanly mentioned in despatches and as casualties of war. Bill Sparks tried valiantly for years to get them a better award, but sadly to no avail.

A BLOODY DISGRACE

After the war, Bill Sparks spent his many post-war working years, happy and contented, as a London bus driver and garage inspector. As if he hadn't already suffered enough at the hands of the authorities, the ungrateful government of the country for which he had fought, and for which his friends had died, dispassionately cut his pension, and in desperation and sadness, he was forced to sell his hard earned medals to prevent losing his retirement home. What an ignominious conclusion!

EPITAPH

This adventure was a joyously happy and monumental time of our lives. It was something that we achieved together as a result of our own volition and alacrity ….. a fond personal memory that no one can eradicate. I was honoured to paddle our canoe as the second most important member of such an illustrious crew. I would say of my wonderful wife Sandra that as well as being naturally endowed with all the positive feminine, diplomatic and compassionate qualities of a woman, she is also a reliably tough, resilient, intelligent and talented partner for any adventure. We compiled this book together using our precious memories of the journey and details from the log books that we kept during the trip.

Roger Downton

I had every confidence in my husband's determination to fulfil his ambition. When things got tough, he persevered using his ingenuity, resourcefulness and willpower to achieve his goal. I'm eternally grateful to him for stoically continuing to paddle when my energy was sapped. I felt proud to be an integral part of the tribute to those brave men, whilst supporting my husband as together we ventured into unknown territory ….. an unforgettable, focused and most enjoyable experience.

Sandra Downton

THE COCKLESHELL HEROES

Roll of Honour

Major Hasler and Marine Bill Sparks
Lieutenant Mackinnon and Marine Conway
Sergeant Wallace and Marine Ewart
Corporal Laver and Marine Mills
Corporal Sheard and Marine Moffat
Marine Ellery and Marine Fisher

REVELATION

The best man at our wedding was my friend from childhood, David Hitchings. Following our expedition, Dave told me that after the war, he often met with Lieutenant-Colonel Hasler when he paid regular visits to his company. Hasler was still busily employed in the boat design industry. After the War, Hasler enjoyed a busy and industrious career in boating design, and in 1956, along with Francis Chichester, created the first transatlantic, single-handed boat challenge. In 1960, Hasler took second place in the race, having crossed the Atlantic alone in forty eight days.

CONGRATULATIONS

Although we received many congratulations, this particular letter arrived from our solicitor in response to a post adventure newspaper article, and was particularly relevant to our theme:

"I was intrigued to read about Operation Frankton and of your fascinating adventure. Congratulations on the achievement and of your enterprise.

One of the reasons why my interest was so aroused is that one of my good friends owns Anderson's Manor which is where, as you probably know, the concept, administration and execution of the project of the Cockleshell Heroes arose.

I remember some years ago my chum telling me that he was out in the grounds one day, and a very, very tall distinguished gentleman in tweed suit and brown brogues approached him and asked if he could look around the house. It turned out that this elderly gent was Lord Head who was, I think, head of Operations at Anderson's during most of the war.

Great to read about you."

….. and this, from my service Commanding Officer:

"Congratulations to you both on your planning, determination and great success in achieving your goal."

General Sir Robert Pascoe, KCB, MBE

LA GIRONDE REVISTED

On a return visit to France and the Bordeaux region some weeks later, we were surprised but happy to be hit by a huge surge of energy emanating from the Gironde area. It felt like home, a welcoming back by the spirits of those gallant warriors, The Cockleshell Heroes. Every time we look at the swirling surface of the milk chocolate Gironde, we have the unnerving feeling of something beckoning us towards it, tempting us to return in our canoe. It's rather like standing on a very tall building and trying to resist that uncanny, illogical urge to jump. We do feel an affinity with the river, but it's a wily old demon and has unfinished business where we are concerned. We half expected to see a mermaid, with sinister intentions, signalling us to return.

THE SUBJECT MATTER

As far as we know, all the information and details regarding the raid are accurate according to the available evidence accessed during our research. We do not profess to be experts on the subject of Operation Frankton, but believe we have produced a true overall presentation.

THANKS

Diana Henderson, Bournemouth Daily Echo, for her articles.

BBC South Today for featuring our daring deed.

Brittany Ferries for our concessionary tickets.

BBC Radio 4 for inviting us as guests on Sandi Toksvig's 'Excess Baggage' programme.